Ripper Hunter

Ripper Hunter

Abberline and the
Whitechapel Murders

M.J. Trow

First published in Great Britain in 2012 by
WHARNCLIFFE TRUE CRIME
An imprint of
Pen & Sword Books Ltd
47 Church Street
Barnsley
South Yorkshire
S70 2AS

Copyright © M.J. Trow

ISBN 978-1-84884-763-7

The right of M.J. Trow to be identified as the author of this work has been
asserted by him in accordance with the Copyright, Designs and Patents Act 1988.

Typeset by Concept, Huddersfield, West Yorkshire
Printed and bound in England by the MPG Books Group, Ltd.

Pen & Sword Books Ltd incorporates the imprints of Pen & Sword Aviation,
Pen & Sword Family History, Pen & Sword Maritime, Pen & Sword Military,
Pen & Sword Discovery, Wharncliffe Local History, Wharncliffe True Crime,
Wharncliffe Transport, Pen & Sword Select, Pen & Sword Military Classics,
Leo Cooper, The Praetorian Press, Remember When, Seaforth Publishing and
Frontline Publishing.

For a complete list of Pen & Sword titles please contact
PEN & SWORD BOOKS LIMITED
47 Church Street, Barnsley, South Yorkshire, S70 2AS, England
E-mail: enquiries@pen-and-sword.co.uk
Website: www.pen-and-sword.co.uk

Contents

List of Plates

OS map of Whitechapel.

Punch – the Burglarian Question, 1886.

Punch – Bull's Eye on Bobby, 1887.

Abberline's Press Cuttings.

Frederick George Abberline's birth certificate.

The Trial of the Dynamitards, 1885.

The Dynamitards, Cunningham and Burton, at their trial in 1885.

Artist's impression of Abberline.

Superintendent Thomas Arnold.

The babyfarmers, Joseph and Annie Roodhouse, in the dock.

The docker's wife, victim of the babyfarmers.

The conman Walter Selwyn, aka Retlaw Nelmes.

The site of the Unicorn Tavern.

The Whitechapel Baths and Wash-house.

Salisbury Street, Blandford Forum.

A clock made by Robert Hood of Blandford.

Hannah Abberline's shop.

New Scotland Yard.

The grave of Frederick and Emma Abberline.

Acknowledgements

My thanks to everyone who contributed to the writing of this book: in particular to Paul Begg for allowing me access to Abberline's reminiscences; Neil Paterson of the Historic Collection, Metropolitan Police for permission to use the Abberline newspaper cuttings; Blandford Town Museum and Bournemouth Library (Archive Section). Especial thanks to Eloise Campbell who has pounded more London pavements taking photographs than Fred Abberline ever did! And most especially to my wife, who is so busy with her own creativity that she does not really have time to type out mine – but she does it anyway.

The Detectives' Rescue

So it isn't by showing his hand,
Or supplying the needs of the Press
With a sketch of the scheme he has plann'd,
That his efforts he'll crown with success;
But by keeping the threads that he's got
To himself, careful no chance to miss.
Well, he tracked out the dynamite plot –
Ten to one he'll make something of this!
But that you'll share his confidence, pray don't expect.
Bear in mind a Detective is meant to *detect!*

Punch or the London Charivari
20 October 1888

Chapter 1

Will the real Inspector Abberline ...?

Chief Inspector Abberline's favourite colour was flesh – especially somebody else's. Especially if that somebody else was the right side of thirty with a figure like the Venus de Milo; before her arms dropped off, of course.

Such a one, alas, was not Mrs Ermintrude Abberline, née Pargeter, of the Neasden Pargeters. She was decidedly the wrong side of thirty, but then it could be argued that Mrs Abberline was the wrong side of everything, especially Chief Inspector Abberline. And flesh was certainly not her colour. Indeed, the last time she had been pestered by the Chief Inspector he had been a detective sergeant and Mr Disraeli was Prime Minister. That had been in 1874.

She faced him that early morning over the marmalade and the toast, wondering what on earth she had seen in the whiskered stranger moronically dunking his rookies in his soft-boiled egg. Once, perhaps, he had been a dashing and undoubtedly white sergeant, at a time when dundrearies were still the height of fashion. Now he, and they, looked a trifle passé.

'That Chinaman called yesterday with your shirts, Frederick,' she said.

'Hmm,' he responded wittily, checking the obituaries in the *Police Gazette*.

'Yes, he was very apologetic.'

'Hmm,' said Abberline, ever one for the dry quip and the variety of response.

1

'He said he and his family had been in the laundry business since the First Opium War and he had never known lipstick stains so stubborn.'

'Lipstick?' Abberline's composure cracked at last. He would rather face the Yard's rubber-truncheon room any day than Mrs Abberline at her most persistent. She made the Spanish Inquisition look like a casual inquiry.

'Yes, Frederick.' She had the pursed lips of the habitual lemon sucker. 'You know, it's the pink stuff that young girls paint on their faces. In my day ...'

'In your day, Ermintrude ...'

'How dare you interrupt me when I'm making a moral and historical observation, Frederick!' she thundered and the windows shook. 'In my day, those females who wore lipstick were harlots. No better than they should be, Frederick. Creatures of the night.'

'Come, come, dearest.' The Chief Inspector folded the *Gazette*. 'This is 1895.'[1]

And by 1895, Frederick Abberline had left the Metropolitan Police Force and was working as a private enquiry agent. He did not have a wife called Ermintrude. Her real name was Emma (née Beament) and we have no idea of the nature of their relationship. The fact that the marriage lasted fifty-three years and only ended with his death, however, is probably evidence enough that it was nothing like the breakfast scenario you have just read.

I embarked on a fiction series in 1985 featuring Inspector Lestrade, the 'best of a bad bunch' of Scotland Yard detectives made to take second place behind Sherlock Holmes by their creator, Arthur Conan Doyle. I was annoyed by the extraordinary arrogance of Holmes and the crawling sycophancy of the Yard men as Doyle wrote it and decided to turn the tables and have Lestrade as the dogged, crime-solving hero and Holmes as a neurotic, drug-addicted amateur. I also decided to mix actual historical characters with fictional and so a whole range of real policemen appear in the sixteen adventures of Lestrade that I wrote.

Abberline was one of them. He was just a name to me then, featuring in the half a dozen books on the Ripper murders that I had then read. I knew he came from Dorset so I dropped in a few references to that. I knew what he looked like from the profile drawing in the papers at the time of the Tower of London bombing in 1885 so I could refer to his huge side whiskers, known as 'Dundrearies' or 'Piccadilly weepers'. Everything else had to be invented because I knew nothing else about the man. As in every other institution, Scotland Yard was riven by internal politics (in 1888 most obviously between the Commissioner, Sir Charles Warren, and his number two, in charge of the CID, James Monro). So I made Abberline an opponent of Lestrade, belittling him at every turn and actively obstructing his enquiries from time to time. Just to underline the fact that Abberline was a thorough-going rotter, I made him a womaniser, playing away from home with a mistress in Penge. The whole of the Yard knew about this and 'Ermintrude' suspected it, so Frederick Abberline was a man who continually looked over his shoulder.

The centenary of the Whitechapel murders was in 1988 and there was a flurry of books on both sides of the Atlantic to mark the fact. There was also a made-for-television movie and its central character was Inspector Frederick Abberline, played by Michael Caine. The four-hour epic, financed by Thames Television and Euston Films, was shown exactly 100 years after the Autumn of Terror when Jack the Ripper stalked the East End, called by journalist Jack London 'the Abyss'. *Jack the Ripper*'s co-writer and producer was David Wickes and a great deal of emphasis was given (in the opening credits) to the fact that new information from Home Office files was being used for the first time. The film was said to have had several different endings made, but in fact it was simply a dramatized account of Stephen Knight's 'highest in the land' theory, with suitable modifications for simplicity of storyline or dramatic effect.

The over-the-top drama comes mostly from the psychic Robert Lees (Ken Bones), who has a disturbing vision of a killer with two faces. The real Lees did (according to his own evidence) offer his services to both the Metropolitan and City Forces in their hunt for the Whitechapel murderer, but he got short shrift, presumably from a cynical desk-sergeant, so a miffed Robert Lees retired from history. There is actually no record of Lees having contacted the police at all,

3

but a psychic who is haunted by ghastly visions makes for excellent television.

With a nod to the American market, the man with two faces turns out in the film to be the New York actor Richard Mansfield (Armande Assante) who is wowing audiences on the London stage with his terrifying Dr Jekyll and Mr Hyde, the study of schizophrenia which Robert Louis Stevenson had written two years earlier. So terrifying was this transformation, according to the film, that it not only made the police suspicious of Mansfield, but the show had to close as it was too frightening. In fact it closed for just the opposite reason – it was not scary enough and the box office returns were dismal. As Denis Meikle says:

> Jack the Ripper has a surface veneer of truth and authority. It appears to have gone to tremendous lengths to recreate the scene of the crimes (and in the case of the crime-scenes themselves, it succeeds) but, underneath, all is trickery and sleight-of-hand; everything about the film is historically overblown and distorted as the fake Richard Mansfield's latex face mask.[2]

The sets are excellent, with real attempts to recreate the physical layout of, for instance, No. 13 Miller's Court, where Mary Jane Kelly died in November 1888. Leaving aside the preposterous central thesis and dénouement – that the Whitechapel murderer was a deranged Sir William Gull, the queen's physician-in-ordinary, killing his targets in a sinister black coach driven by the megalomaniac John Netley, 'that's Dr Netley, in actual fact' – other characters are distorted to fit the mood of the 1980s. Most 'off the wall' of all is the persona of George Lusk. Lusk was, in reality, a builder, specializing in music-hall restoration, who was declared bankrupt twice. In 1888 his wife died and he was left to bring up seven children. In the film, Michael Gothard plays him as a Marxist anarchist, conspiring with the Press to attack the establishment and urging the flaming torch-carrying mob to storm Scotland Yard itself. We even have a few strains of The Red Flag to underline the point. In fact, Lusk was a Freemason and did his best to be a pillar of the establishment. He chaired the Whitechapel Vigilance Committee because he believed the police needed help. Anyone less likely to take to the barricades would be hard to find.

4

What of the police in *Jack the Ripper*? The interiors of Leman Street police station and the Yard are excellent, with wooden filing cabinets and all the clutter that the 'old' Scotland Yard must have had. Among the uniformed men (all of whom, according to their collar insignia, are from J Division[3] and not H for Whitechapel and Spitalfields as they should have been) there are the usual stereotypes. The constable known only as Derek (Gary Love) is young, clean-cut and honest. Tell him what to do and he'll do it, but don't expect initiative or quick-thinking. This is probably a fair portrayal of the rank and file of the Metropolitan Police in 1888. Sergeant Kirby (Peter Armitage) is a scruffy, disorganized lout, but only because he has Inspector John Spratling (Jon Laurimore) as his role model. The film's Spratling hates Abberline with a passion – the man has, after all, come back from the lofty heights of Scotland Yard to oversee the case – and there is a hint of a long-standing feud between them. The real Spratling claimed that he smoked blacker tobacco and drank blacker tea than anybody in the Met; if this was so, it didn't do him much harm – he died aged ninety-three in 1938! Ironically, given Spratling's good record, Henry Kirby was demoted to constable for drinking in a pub on 27 October 1888 at the height of the Ripper scare, so perhaps the film's portrayal of him is not so wide of the mark.

Superintendent Arnold (Edward Judd), who ran H Division, is portrayed as difficult and unhelpful to Abberline – the real man backed him all the way and said that losing Abberline to retirement was like losing his right hand. The portrayal of Sir Charles Warren (Hugh Fraser) is extraordinary and unique in the Ripper films. He may have been a competent amateur archaeologist, even a creditable soldier (before 1888, not afterwards)[4], but as Commissioner, he was a disaster. Fraser plays him as a beleaguered hero, the victim of the Press and the mob. Certainly, the Press despised the real Warren, largely because of his mishandling of the 'Bloody Sunday' riots in Trafalgar Square in 1887, but most policemen had a grudging respect for him and it is this aspect that perhaps comes across in the film.

The heroes of course are Abberline and Godley, the latter played by screen tough-guy Lewis Collins. He is cynical and worldly wise, but very loyal to his 'guv'nor'. His clothes are extremely dapper and he gets involved in pub 'punch-ups' in the way that Metropolitan policemen often did. The teaming of Godley and Abberline is pure fiction, however. Crime fiction, on the large and small screens and in novels, often revolves around an inspector and his sergeant. Their relationships differ, but they are there largely as mutual sounding boards for theories to move the plot along. The real Godley was a sawyer before joining the Met and ended up as the inspector who arrested Severin Klosowski, aka George Chapman, for the murder of his wives in 1903. He certainly worked with Abberline, in that both men attended the inquest on Ripper victim Mary Ann Nichols, but since he was in J Division it is not likely that he was part of the inner circle who ran the case under Abberline.

What can we make of Michael Caine's Abberline? There is no attempt to portray him as a Dorsetman; in fact there are various references in the script to East-Enders being 'my people'; his old dad, Caine tells us, 'was a blacksmith' – actually Abberline's father was a saddler. Caine is always a presence on the screen and hardly squares with Walter Dew's famous description of Abberline as looking like a bank manager. Caine snarls and spits his way through the film, fully aware of the powerful opposition to him in the corridors of power. He is tough, honest, practical, not averse to strong-arm tactics and conveys very well the sheer frustration of a detective who is making little or no progress. None of the film's suspects were actually in the frame except the 'mad pork butcher' Jacob Isenschmid (John Dair), who appears on screen for seconds and is released from gaol because he is left-handed! What is unforgivable is that Abberline is characterized as an alcoholic. The first time we meet him he is sleeping off a binge in a police cell. He keeps bottles of Scotch in his filing cabinet and the ever-devoted Godley is on hand to make sure his 'guv'nor' doesn't fall off the wagon during the investigation. Drunkenness was certainly a major issue for the Victorians – one of the social evils that various Temperance societies were trying to combat – and it was an on-going problem for the police, but there isn't a shred of evidence that Abberline drank. Inevitably, in the course of his enquiries into East End crime he spent time in various East End pubs, but that merely went with the territory.

But if Michael Caine's Abberline had a vice, Johnny Depp's version of 2001 has them all! Just as *Jack the Ripper* was locked into a variant of the Stephen Knight theory involving the highest in the land, *From Hell* was taken from the graphic novel which went all out for the royal conspiracy theory. Given that starting point, it was all expert Ripper historians Keith Skinner and Stewart Evans, working as technical advisers, could do to keep the story relatively near the truth.

Denis Meickle defines the graphic novel as:

> stylistically occupying a halfway house between novel and film. Graphic novels are the products of artists raised on the moving image, rather than the static tableaux of conventional illustration.[5]

It looks like a film story board, flashing backwards and forwards with 'reality' and dream sequences merging. *From Hell*, written by Alan Moore and drawn by Eddie Campbell and Pete Mullins, was 'a melodrama in sixteen parts'. 'The result,' wrote Patrick Day in *The Los Angeles Times* 'is at once a meditation on evil, a police procedural and a commentary on Victorian England.' As a piece of historical research, however, it is deeply flawed. Alan Moore admits as much in his Appendix I, which is a detailed annotation of the chapters. Where Moore was quite brilliant was in working real historical facts and scenarios into the fiction and in drawing on the researches of some of the finest Ripper experts around.[6]

Moore sums up his position in a scene between Abberline and his wife, Emma. The words spoken between them:

> are completely without justification and are entirely based upon my own view of the man, constructed from the relatively few surviving details pertaining to his life. As with so much of *From Hell*, when we know the details of a person's life but not how he or she felt, then we must resort to fiction unless we are to exclude feelings altogether, which I don't feel inclined to do.[7]

I can't afford the luxury! Moore is absolutely right. Throughout the snippets of Abberline's life which are available, there is *nothing* to tell us how he felt. We can make some guarded assumptions based on the generalities of human nature, but the past, as L.P.

Hartley reminded us, 'is a foreign country: they do things differently there.' It is likely that Frederick Abberline fumed when he could not net the big fish in the Cleveland Street scandal; kicked himself metaphorically when he failed to find Jack the Ripper; perhaps he cried over the murdered body of little Fanny Lazarus – but we simply do not know.

The film of the book is inevitably simplified but, unlike the Michael Caine version, takes Stephen Knight's 'highest in the land' theory to its ultimate conclusion, with a cameo appearance by Queen Victoria herself. Again the villain is a suitably 'barking' William Gull, but this time he is backed by a Masonic order that is sinister, all-powerful and includes Sir Charles Warren (Ian Richardson at his most repellent!). There is far more focus here on the Ripper's victims, all of whom (because the storyline demands it) know each other. We have no information on this. The Abyss of Whitechapel and Spitalfields was a small area, but nearly half a million people crowded its mean streets and no details on the victims' connection with each other have been found. There is too much cleavage shown for 1880s reality – such low-cut bodices belong to the balls and soirées of the rich and fashionable West End; Victorian street women just did not dress that way. And why Elizabeth Stride is given lesbian tendencies is not explained, other than to add pointless titillation.

The sense of Victorian London is less impressive than in the Caine film, with the usual dark corners, flashing steel and grimy interiors. The sets alone cost $1 million, but they were built on a site in Prague and fail to convince. The mortuary (presumably the Whitechapel Workhouse Infirmary in Eagle Place, off Old Montague Street) is vast, cavernous and fan-vaulted – in reality it was little more than a shed. Incomprehensibly, the police surgeon (played by Ian McNeice) vomits at the sight of his victim on the slab; real police surgeons were made of sterner stuff and the majority of them did an excellent job bearing in mind the limits of forensic knowledge of the time.

Denis Meickle sums up the film as a whole: '*From Hell* is the Whitechapel killings as they never were but as they might be were they to have been researched by Charles Berlitz or Whitley Streiber ...'[8]

It does not pretend to be realistic, but a fantasy evoking terror and evil. Geography is ignored. William Gull crosses the Thames in his carriage to get from his address in Brooke Street, Mayfair, to Whitechapel (a *very* long way round) and, as with the 1988 *Jack* there is no sense of the jurisdiction issues in the murder of Kate Eddowes. The City Police get no mention at all and Abberline swans around the place without observing any of the inter-constabulary protocol.

Once again, what of the police? There is much less play on them than in the Michael Caine version. They are there as back-up for the detectives, actually, at two points in the film, forming a dense, blue-coated and anonymous audience at one of Abberline's briefing sessions. There is one telling scene where a patrolling constable 'moves on' Abberline and Mary Kelly in a clinch before realizing who Abberline is. It is unhistorical fiction, but it is nicely done, the constable realizing that Abberline is far above him in the chain of command. In fact, there is no chain of command. Abberline reports directly to Sir Charles Warren. There is no Superintendent Arnold of H Division, no Chief Inspector Donald Swanson at the Yard; no Monro in overall charge of the CID; just Warren, who is totally antagonistic from his first appearance. Photographs are taken at every murder site – perhaps in reality they were, but only two have survived, both taken in Mary Kelly's room in Miller's Court.

Sergeant Godley – for some reason called Peter rather than George – is played by Robbie Coltrane. He is as fond of Abberline as Lewis Collins was in the 1988 film. He is also erudite, quoting Plato and Shakespeare to explain the madness around him. One cannot be judgmental about these things – Godley reached undying fame later as the man who arrested multiple murderer Severin Klosowski – but the fact that he was a manual labourer before he joined the Met militates the likelihood of the quotations.

But it is Abberline himself who is the most over-the-top character in the film. It opens with the inspector smoking a pipe in an opium den and having to be fished out by Godley and a few lads in uniform who are told to turn a metaphorical blind eye. Throughout the film, Abberline sees visions, though whether these are drug-induced or examples of his own psychic abilities is not quite clear. He 'sees' the murders in advance, so actual police procedure, of knocking on doors and asking questions, is not really necessary. In that sense,

Depp's Abberline is his own Robert Lees. When the film was released, Depp was interviewed on television and admitted that he played the Inspector as a Cockney (which he does to perfection) because he couldn't do a Dorset accent. Unlike the Caine version, where Abberline has no social or home life whatever except for a vague fling with a fictional artist played by Jane Seymour, we learn that Depp's character had a wife, Victoria (actually, Martha) and that she and her baby died in childbirth. Martha Mackness was Abberline's first wife and she died of tuberculosis only two months after their wedding. There was no child.

Being single, however, does give Depp's Abberline a chance to build up a relationship with Mary Kelly (played by Heather Graham). When he finally realizes the extent of the Masonic plot that has led to the slaughter of the Whitechapel women, he pins Sir Charles Warren against a wall in Miller's Court, which most of the 'bobbies' milling around don't seem to notice. He finds grape stems near the victims' bodies, consults Dr Gull as in the Stephen Knight version, and is intensely relieved to discover that Mary Kelly is not dead, and that a vague lookalike died in her place. Such was the extent of the mutilations in the Kelly murder that the girl's face was unrecognizable and the real Abberline spent some time interviewing a local woman called Caroline Maxwell, who swore she had talked to Mary Kelly some six hours after she died. Out of what was probably a genuine mistake on Maxwell's part, all sorts of conspiracy theories can be woven.

Abberline's death in the opium den was a shock when the film first appeared. It was also totally unnecessary. Mary Kelly was safe at home in Ireland. William Gull was a vegetable in his own lunatic asylum. The conspiracy was over. But Depp's Abberline is a tragic hero in the Shakespearean mould. He has solved the crimes but can never admit it for fear of having the Masons renew their hunt for Mary and in the end the world, of Masonic conspiracy and drug addiction, is more powerful than he is.

In 2010 Hugo Weaving played Abberline in a horror flick called *The Wolfman*. Alone among actors who have played him, Weaving wore the derby hat and sidewhiskers, but the cast list has him as Francis Aberline and while one website article claims that 'Francis' was the real Abberline's nickname, the only use of the name is in a single newspaper account from 1878 where it is, in all probability, a mistake. Other policemen certainly have *noms de guerre*, largely given to them by the underworld; Frederick Wensley, a young constable in Abberline's day, was Mr Weasel (or Wenzel to the Jewish community); Walter Dew was 'Blue Serge' (after his suit); William Thick was 'Johnny Upright' (because of his bearing and honesty); Eli Caunter was 'Tommy Roundhead'.

But there appears to have been no nickname for Abberline.

In the world of cyber-lunacy, Abberline has a vampire alter-ego in the form of DI Boyd (played by Trevor Eve) in *Waking the Dead*. It just gets sillier and sillier ... All of us who have hijacked Frederick Abberline, whether we are novelists, actors, screenplay writers, directors or producers, are all guilty to a greater or lesser extent of misrepresenting the man. This book sets out to put the record straight.

Chapter 2

The Clocksmith from Blandford

'It matters not where my father fed his flocks,' wrote Chief Inspector John Littlechild in the *Reminiscences* he wrote in 1894; but in fact it matters very much. Inspectors of Scotland Yard do not leap fully-formed into the battle against crime and Littlechild's upbringing, like Abberline's, made him the man – and detective – he was.

Frederick George Abberline was born in the bitter January of 1843 in Blandford Forum, on a bend in the River Stour in Dorset. In that year, Isambard Kingdom Brunel's SS *Great Britain* was launched, then the largest ship in the world. Charles Dickens wrote *A Christmas Carol* in serial form and John Horsley designed the first Christmas card. The philosopher John Stuart Mill wrote *The System of Logic* and William Wordsworth, the Lake poet, was made Laureate.

But Abberline was born into the 'hungry forties', a period of grim recession alleviated only slightly by the railway boom that would not reach Blandford as a stopping-off point until the year he left home (1863). The queen was Victoria. She was twenty-four years old and had ruled England for six years, the last three with the help and support of the able and loyal Prince Albert of Saxe-Coburg Gotha. By the time Abberline was born, the royal couple had two children, with a third on the way, and had just bought the Osborne estate in the Isle of Wight as a retreat from the cares of state. Victoria's Prime Minister was Robert Peel who, as Home Secretary fourteen years earlier, had founded the Metropolitan Police in which Abberline would make his name. The tall, shy 'gentleman of business' had not yet destroyed his career and his party. The first Prime Minister in years to understand figures and have a good grasp of the economy, Peel was busy freeing up trade and helping to create the 'workshop of the world' image, in which Britain would bask throughout the 1850s and 1860s. Steam and steel, iron and cotton, railways and the constant rhythm of machines were what the 1840s were all about. They were also about low wages, high unemployment and marches by men who demanded the six points of the People's Charter and were determined to end the vicious economic dictatorship of the 'field of corn'.

How much of this growing class consciousness permeated through to the rural backwater of Dorset is debatable. The county was lit with a national spotlight when seven labourers from the village of Tolpuddle were transported to Van Diemen's Land for 'administering illegal oaths' (actually, for daring to join a trade union). It would be another thirty years before farm labourers tried again, miles to the north in Warwickshire. It is likely that Tolpuddle set the seal on the power of the landowning classes for the whole of Abberline's childhood. When Fred Abberline was five Karl Marx and Friedrich Engels wrote *The Communist Manifesto*, advocating worldwide revolution; but it would be forty years before an English translation of the original German appeared and by that time Abberline was local inspector in charge of the Criminal Investigation Department in Whitechapel in London's East End.

In country areas like Dorset, dotted with dozens of villages and small market towns, most people looked back, not forward, and were probably less aware of the gathering momentum of change than we are today. To the south of Blandford lie villages like Winterbourne Stickland and Charlton Marshall. The honey-coloured stone that made the houses blended with the rolling countryside at harvest time. Some twenty miles away at Cerne Abbas, the giant carved into the chalk was already 1,500 years old, but there was now a discreet bush growing over the pagan fertility symbol's immense penis so that middle-class sensibilities would not be offended. Between Blandford and the county town of Dorchester lay the land that Thomas Hardy (a boy of three at the time of Abberline's birth) would make famous in his Wessex novels years later.

The market town of Blandford Forum, also called Cheping Blandford, was held, according to William I's Domesday Book in 1086, by Bretel for his overlord the Count of Mortain. In the time of King Edward (i.e. before 1066) it was held by the Saxon Alweard. 'It

14

paid geld for 1½ hides. There is land for 1 plough. It renders 12s. It was worth 20s.'[1] Other parts of the town were held by William de Eu. His demesne included one plough with three slaves and three bordars.[2] And yet more belonged to Ainulf, who held it directly from the king. His land included five acres of meadow and two furlongs of pasture. The relative prosperity of medieval Blandford was disturbed several times by fire, always a real danger in settlements built of timber, wattle and daub. The first of these in the early modern period struck the town in 1579, but worse followed in 1677, 1713 and 1731, after which virtually the whole place had to be rebuilt. The royal family (George II was king at the time) sent a total of £1,300 into what today would be classified a disaster area and Blandford emerged, phoenix-like, as a brand new Georgian town, complete with wide streets and imposing buildings.

Much of Blandford's importance at the time of Abberline's birth derived from its position. It was 104 miles from London on the great road (now the A354) that ran to Weymouth, Exeter and Plymouth and acted as an important staging post to change horses in the days of coach travel. A traveller's guide of 1831 lists thirty-one pubs, many of which would have been hotels where food, drink and beds for the night were available. The church of St Peter and St Paul dominated the main street with its ornate Baroque tower 105 feet high. There was even a small chapel nearby for Catholics, just to show that the people of Blandford Forum were as tolerant as the next parish. There were seven schools, including a Bluecoat establishment for twelve boys who were apprenticed to local craftsmen after three years. Dotted around the town were numerous gentlemen's country seats, usually Georgian buildings with stable-wings at the centre of acres of good arable farmland, more enclosed and manicured than anything Bretel or William or Ainulf would have known. 'The air is most salubrious,' said the travellers' guide, and reminded passers-through that market day was Saturday and the emphasis was on cheese, cattle and sheep. Fairs, probably medieval in origin, were held on 7 March, 19 July and 8 November.

Ten years after the travellers' guide was written, the Abberline family appear on the 1841 census. This was only the third taken in the country's history and it was inevitably prone to error. Like everything else in Abberline's story, we can only go with the written

15

record, often fragmented and occasionally contradictory. At that time the Abberlines were living in Salisbury Street, where the fire of 1731 had broken out. It was one of Blandford's major thoroughfares and the family consisted of five people. Edward Abberline was head of the household. He was aged forty and was a saddler by trade. In a semi-rural area where horses were a way of life, for transport, hunting and draught work, the job must have kept him busy and with a steady income. He was also, in a small community where everyone knew everyone else and status was all, a sheriff's officer and a clerk for the town markets. These may be important pointers in his son's future career. The Abberlines were literate, took their role in society seriously and already had links with the law. Hannah (née Chinn), his wife, was Edward's age and ten years later would be running a shop. Whether she was already doing so in 1841 we do not know, but certainly the children; Emily, aged five, Harriet, aged three and Edward junior, aged two, were too young to add to the family income. Tragedy and a move had marked the Abberlines already. Since Emily was born in Salisbury, we can reasonably assume the family hailed from there. Edward and Hannah's first-born, Elizabeth, was born there too in 1834, but she was clearly dead by 1841, a victim of the high infant mortality of the period.

Of Frederick's birth and early life we know nothing. Thomas Hardy, born three years earlier in High Bockhampton outside Dorchester, has a much better chronicled Dorset childhood because he became world famous as a writer and incorporated early reminiscences into his novels and poetry. All we can say about little Frederick is that he had hazel eyes! The 1840s was the first decade in which chloroform or ether could be used to dull the pain of childbirth, but it was the queen herself who made chloroform popular and it is likely that Hannah Abberline, surrounded by women of the town and female relatives with a motley smattering of old wives' tales, would simply have gripped the brass bedstead and got on with it. Hot hip baths were sometimes recommended if the labour was difficult, but having borne at least four children before Frederick, Hannah could be said to be well prepared. On the other hand, at forty-two, she was taking a huge risk giving birth at all. The boy would have been born at home, his father kept strictly away from the bedroom, waiting for the traditional slap and cry that heralded the baby's arrival. Most doctors and midwives at the time recommended breastfeeding as the most natural way to feed a baby, although milk bottles with rubber teats had been available for over a decade. The notion of wrapping a newborn infant in tight swaddling clothes had all but disappeared, whatever the Bible said about baby Jesus, and mothers were encouraged to cuddle their bundles of joy as much as possible.

We have no idea what childhood diseases Frederick suffered from, what toys he played with or what books he read. He may have been spoiled by his big sister – he would certainly have worn his big brother's hand-me-down clothes.[3] We have no sure idea either of the strictness of his upbringing. Mothers and fathers both regularly beat their children into obedience, sometimes with a slipper or belt. Children were expected to behave, to accept their situation and to know their station in life. The Abberlines, at the top of the working-class hierarchy, as a saddler and perhaps shopkeeper, as sheriff's officer and market clerk, would have looked down on the farm labourers who gathered in the pubs in their smocks on market days. But Edward senior would have touched his cap brim to the squire, the parson and probably the bank manager and the teacher.

When he was five, Frederick would have been sent to one of the schools in Blandford. Unless his parents set great store by education and were willing to pay fees for private education, this would probably have been the National School in Damary Lane. Even here there was a small fee – there would be no 'free' education until the Ragged Schools in the 1850s and they were only for the very poor. Here, Frederick would learn his times tables and his ABC, and the copperplate handwriting in which he would write his reports on the Ripper killings and his reminiscences of the casinos at Monte Carlo. Then ... the unthinkable. Edward Abberline, the saddler, died.

The sudden loss of a breadwinner was an appalling blow in a society which had no welfare state and no financial safety net. The 1851 census records the now fifty-year-old Hannah as head of the family, living over her shop in East Street. The building still stands, with its dormer window set into the roof and its small bow-fronted panes. Harriet was twelve by now, technically an adult in many ways, and would have helped her mother behind the counter. Edward was eleven and may have left school. Of Emily, who would have been fifteen, there is no mention, but curiously she appears as a servant in 1853 where her age is given (wrongly) as seventeen. It is likely that she was already living in in that capacity with a well-to-do Blandford family in 1851.

The literature of the time is full of sudden riches-to-rags stories. Several of Dickens's sentimental serials, hugely popular throughout the 1840s and 1850s, hinge on it and the social commentator Henry Mayhew cites many examples in his exposé of London poverty written in 1851. The end of that road was the workhouse, with its grim Bastille-like reputation, its rigid repression and ghastly food, but the Abberlines never fell that far. There is no mention of Hannah marrying again and the 1861 census lists her as a sixty-year-old widow, 'formerly shopkeeper', so she may have been reliant on her now grown-up children for survival.

It would be expected that boys would follow their father's line of work, but the early death of Edward senior meant that the saddlery business came to an end. Hannah's two unmarried sons are listed in 1861, but neither of them had followed their father. At twenty-one, Edward was already a man in the eyes of the law, still living at East Street and a cabinet maker. Frederick, three years younger, was a clock and watchmaker.

The usual pattern for boys of young Abberline's social class was to leave school at ten with a basic grounding in the three Rs (the fact that the future Inspector Abberline had no more than a passing acquaintance with French rules out anything more fancy) and become an apprentice. The full term of this was seven years and by the 1850s apprentices no longer lived in with their masters but stayed at home and went to work on a daily basis. We have no idea why Abberline chose watch and clockmaking as a profession, or indeed whether it was strictly his choice. The work required patience, good eyesight and a steady hand and at the end of his apprenticeship Frederick would produce his masterpiece, a fully-functioning timepiece, and could put up his shingle outside his premises and hope he would get custom. It is possible that the clocksmith he worked under was Robert Hood, a widower by 1861 who had a workshop in White Cliff Mill Street. There are two clocks made by Hood in the excellent town museum and a daguerreotype of the man with his grandchild sitting on his knee.

The pen-portrait of Abberline in the incomparable *Jack the Ripper A–Z* says that he served for thirty-five days in the militia. The militia were part-time infantry who effectively replaced the Trained Bands of the Civil War period. In 1757 the Militia Act made military service compulsory at the start of yet another dynastic and trade war with France. Each county had to supply able-bodied young men by ballot, although substitutes were permissible if they could be found. By 1852 a further Act of Parliament made it a volunteer force and all over the country new units were set up in the face of a French invasion. The Crimean War (1853–56) was a rare example of Anglo-French cooperation against a common enemy – Russia – but the norm for a thousand years had been hostility between those countries. Only with hindsight were the state-of-the-art forts in the Solent called Palmerston's Follies. Between 1859 and 1861 the threat of French invasion looked very real. Was Abberline caught up in a burst of patriotic fervour? He was only eighteen in 1861 – in today's terms still a 'sixth former' – and may have got carried away by the recruiting posters. Dorset had a long and proud history of standing by to repel the French – its residents had watched from their coastline throughout the long summer of 1804 for Napoleon Bonaparte – and local folklore may have played its part. Two of Thomas Hardy's novels are set in this period.

Why precisely Abberline joined, where exactly he served and what he did in terms of basic training and 'war games' we do not know. Virtually all the relevant papers of the Dorset Militia were lost to water damage in their store in the 1920s and the name of Frederick Abberline appears nowhere.

One thing is certain; on 5 January 1863, three days before his twentieth birthday, Abberline swapped his scarlet militia uniform for a dark blue one and joined the Metropolitan Police.

Chapter 3

The Boy in Blue

Because Frederick Abberline never wrote anything approximating to a full autobiography, we have no idea why he became a policeman, still less an officer in London's Metropolitan force. Since the Constabulary Act of 1856, every county had to have a police force and Dorset was no exception; in fact, it had been formed the previous year. Perhaps Abberline had relatives in the capital; perhaps he had heard there were excellent career prospects in the Met; perhaps he believed the streets of London were paved with gold. We just do not know.

The Met was thirty-four years old in 1863 and it had been the brainchild of Sir Robert Peel, whose own career – and life – had come to an end when Frederick Abberline was seven, as a result of a fall from his horse. As Home Secretary in 1828, Peel was concerned to clamp down on what was undoubtedly a crime wave in the capital. He had already tackled the criminal law, removing the over-the-top death penalty from nearly 200 offences. He had also introduced his Gaols Act, which saw turnkeys paid for the first time and the concept of rehabilitation introduced into British prisons. By creating a Police for the Metropolis he was taking his biggest risk yet. On the Continent (and in Paris in particular) the police were seen as the government's private army, bent on restricting freedoms that men had held for centuries. There were huge problems to be overcome. The new police must not look like soldiers – hence the swallowtail coats and stove-pipe 'civilian' hats. They must be paid enough to prevent bribe-taking, but not so much that the public – unconvinced of the need for them anyway – would refuse to pay via taxation and rates.

Peel argued long and hard against the diehard reactionaries of his own Tory party and against the radicals outside parliament who warned of a police state without actually using the term. And the Home Secretary would not be shaken. The old constables of the watch, or 'Charlies' as they were known, were mostly decrepit pensioners to whom a warm coat and a lantern for night work were luxuries. Their chances of actually catching a criminal were slim indeed. Peel's Bill became law on 19 June 1829. The new police headquarters were at 4 Whitehall Place, the back door of which opened onto the area where visitors from the north had been housed in the reign of James I – Scotland Yard. Two Justices of the Peace, Richard Mayne and Charles Rowan, were sworn in as Commissioners to work directly under Peel and London was divided into Districts denoted by letters of the alphabet, each run by a superintendent. Under the superintendent came inspectors, sergeants (the only rank lifted from the army) and constables. The City of London, with its own ancient law enforcement, remained separate, as, at first, did the River Police and the Horse Patrols.

It did not go swimmingly. Of the first 3,000 recruits, nearly all were dismissed within eighteen months for drunkenness and/or bribe-taking. Even honest citizens resented their presence, seeing no need for a 'preventative police'. They were spat at in the street and roughed up. The public called them 'blue devils' and 'Peel's raw lobsters' and when one of them, Constable Joseph Grantham of S Division, was kicked to death trying to break up a fight in June 1830, the coroner's jury cleared his murderer, ruling that Grantham had brought about his own death by 'over-exertion in the discharge of his duty'[1]. Three years later, when Constable Robert Culley was fatally stabbed in a riot in Clerkenwell, the coroner's jury returned a verdict of 'justifiable homicide' and a mob jeered the mourners at his funeral.

In the thirty years that intervened before Abberline's joining the police, a certain acceptance of them had crept in and, in central London at least, the crime rate had fallen. Abberline was just the sort of recruit the Met were looking for. 'Agricultural' men were preferred because of their more robust physique, but at five feet eight inches, Abberline was a little on the short side for a man who was expected to hold his own in punch-ups and riot situations. Local men were considered less impressive because of the London smog they had breathed all their lives, and because they were more likely to have criminal associations which might compromise their position.

When Abberline retired from the force in 1892 he explained his lack of memoirs by reminding everybody that his superiors did not approve of them and that officers who had gone into print had been reprimanded. The next generation of detectives did it gleefully: Fred Wensley wrote *Forty Years of Scotland Yard*; Robert Higgins penned *In the Name of the Law*; and George Du Rose published *Murder Was My Business*. But two of Abberline's contemporaries who did go into print – Chief Inspector John Littlechild and Inspector Maurice Moser – are very disappointing in their accounts of their early careers in uniform. Littlechild skates over his with an aside on how nursemaids admired the uniform (he joined the Met four years after Abberline) and Moser does not refer to it at all.

Recruits spent two weeks at Wellington Barracks near Buckingham Palace and were taught a variant of army drill with which Abberline must already have been familiar. They learned to obey orders instantly, and to walk at a regulation 2½ miles an hour. They were taught to use their fourteen-inch hardwood truncheons, but only in self-defence, and cutlass drill should a riot situation get out of hand. After that, it was out on the streets, where the real education started.

Constable 544N Frederick Abberline was posted to N Division and given the warrant number 43519. Patrolling the streets of Islington he was among the last generation of beat policemen to wear the swallowtail coat and stovepipe hat of the original Peelers. Within months, the coat had been replaced by a dark blue tunic, fastened centrally with eight white metal buttons, and dark blue trousers to match.[2] Until 1869 this uniform had to be worn even while an officer was off duty. A broad leather belt carried the truncheon and a bull's eye lantern for night work could be hooked onto it. For communication, Constable Abberline would have carried a wooden rattle, the ratchet teeth of which could be heard, when swung, streets away. Not until 1885 would the famous Metropolitan whistle replace it. Most distinctive of all was the new headgear, a tall 'coxcomb' helmet of infantry pattern with a metal plate at the front. Littlechild says that the wearing of facial hair was forbidden, but the Crimean War, with its intense cold, had made

23

beards and mutton-chop whiskers fashionable and certainly photo-graphs of the period show all types of hirsuteness. This was stand-ardized by Police Orders in 1869 allowing beards and moustaches.

The street job was learned on the spot, young Abberline in tandem with an older hand who showed him the ropes. The beat patrol system which Abberline learned had not changed materially since 1829. In inner London, the beat was 1 to 1½ miles, but in more rural areas like Islington it was often longer. The size of the beat and the pace of patrolling meant that each officer would in theory visit any part of it every fifteen minutes. Abberline would have had his 'appointments' (rattle and truncheon) checked by the station sergeant before marching off with seven colleagues to a point at which his beat began. Once patrolling, he could not talk to another officer except in an emergency; neither could he smoke or enter a pub. There were no refreshment breaks, so Abberline would have been sensible to pack some bread and cheese into his pockets before the stint began. Answering the call of nature would almost certainly have been on an ad hoc basis, behind any handy tree. The whole operation was timed using a beat wheel, a contraption that measured exact distance, and Abberline would have been expected to meet up with his sergeant at a fixed point on the street to report incidents or to report that all was well. At night, patrols checked locks and doorways, moving on drunks and breaking up fights. Abberline would have got to know the local bad boys (and girls) and would have written up reports on incidents in his copperplate handwriting for the station sergeant. N Division covered sixty square miles and was always one of the largest, both in terms of size and the number of officers.

Islington was one of the 'villages' of London until the 1820s, when it was incorporated into the ever-expanding 'wen', as William Cobbett called the capital. The invention of Edwin Shilibeer's omnibus and the digging of the Regent's Canal to Limehouse turned Islington into suburbia. But whereas the genteel settled there in solid, respectable terraces, the demolition of slums in central London to build railway termini meant that a steady trickle of the poor and criminal classes moved there as well. The archery butts and the gardens and ponds with wild ducks gave way to red brick Victoriana. Islington Green already had a reputation before they

built an imposing statue to Hugh Myddleton, who had brought a
fresh water supply to the area via the River Lea in the early seventeenth century. In fact the statue was brand new when Constable
Abberline patrolled past it. The ever-watchful satirical magazine
Punch wrote of the Green in 1847:

> They say Pitch-and-Toss sinful
>   Resorts to my ground;
> That here sorts, with a skinful,
>   Reclining are found.
> If rogues seek to fleece men
>   Or topers to sleep,
> All I want's two policemen
>   My confines to keep.[3]

The Metropolitan cattle market was erected in Islington in 1855,
replacing Smithfield as London's major meat market. The Royal
Agricultural Hall was built the year before Abberline arrived and
may well have reminded him of home. Music halls and theatres
sprang up around the Green, the newest of them, Collins's, setting
up shop in 1862.

We have no idea of Abberline's precise beat, in which station he
was based or where he lived, but as an unmarried officer, it would
have been in the grim confines of a Station House. These were often
built alongside a police station so that as many men as possible
would be available at short notice in the event of a riot situation.
Furniture consisted of a hard bed, a fold-down table and a dining
chair. Toilets were an open row of troughs without any privacy
and there was no hot water. Not until the 1930s would anything
approaching comfort be brought into these spartan establishments.
Combine this with the low pay, the exhausting miles pounding a
beat and the stressful mix of long hours of boredom punctuated by
bursts of high-adrenaline action and it is difficult to see why young
men like Abberline stayed in the job at all.

Perhaps, in a simpler age, it was the oath Abberline took which
meant something to him:

> I swear that I will well and truly to the best of my knowledge
> and ability act as a Constable for the Metropolitan Police district

... for preserving the Peace and preventing Robberies and other Felonies and apprehending offenders against the Peace ... so help me God.

Only once during his time with N Division does Abberline appear in the Press. His name was misspelt Albertine, but that was something he would have to get used to. The offence, in September 1864, was a misdemeanour involving fireworks. 'Squibs' had always been regarded as dangerous – they still are – and carried a stiff prison sentence until the 1820s when Robert Peel recodified various crimes to bring them in line with nineteenth-century reality. Within three years, the use of explosives on London streets would assume an altogether more terrifying aspect in the hands of the Fenians.

When we next hear of Abberline, arresting a violent thug called John Fleet, he is Police Sergeant 24Y and times have already changed. His promotion came in August 1865 while still with N Division, so clearly he had impressed his superiors after only two and a half years on the job. The pay improved, of course, and he now wore three silver thread chevrons on his tunic sleeves. One of about sixteen sergeants in the Division, his principal role was to supervise the day to day work of constables, eight of whom were out on patrol and the ninth, in reserve, waiting at the station. Abberline's 'manor' was the entire beat area his men patrolled and it was now his job to check their appointments, before marching out with them to their positions. He would still patrol himself, carrying out his own checks as well as monitoring what his men were doing. This element of policing, in line with Peel's notion of a 'preventive police', gave reassurance to the public as the 'bobbie' turned slowly into a symbol of comfort and trust.

Two months later Abberline was posted to Y Division (newly created in 1865) in the northern borough of Highgate. The move was probably to allow a keen and competent young man to get on; Abberline was still only twenty-two and could be looking at another thirty years on the force. Highgate was even more of a village than Islington. This was the spot where, according to legend, Dick Whittington paused and heard the bells of London calling him back to become Lord Mayor in the fourteenth century. An impressive stone bridge across the gorge was opened in 1813, but what dominated the area was the vast necropolis inaugurated in 1839. The great and the good of mid-Victorian society were buried there among mausoleums as weird and wonderful as they were Gothic, and while Abberline was a sergeant in the Division, the physicist Michael Faraday joined the happy throng of the dead.

Y Division was smaller than N Division, both in terms of geographical area and numbers of men. The range of crimes that Abberline was involved with in the years up to his next transfer in 1873 was in many ways a microcosm of London's skulduggery. In September 1870, he charged Edward George with assault. The following April there was a similar case involving Arthur Fulsham. In the August of 1871 John Heddy and Walter Gold were arrested for purse-stealing and the next month Henry Muggeridge was charged with forging cheques. This was Abberline's first appearance at the Central Criminal Court, better known as the Old Bailey. Forgery and fraud cases were notoriously difficult to prosecute and Muggeridge got off.

One of the most interesting cases that came Abberline's way happened in August 1872 when he arrested three women – Elizabeth and Maria Sullivan and Jane Adams – for disorderly conduct and dressing in male attire. Details of these early cases are very sketchy. Routine investigations like these were logged and written up longhand – it would be several years after its standardization in the 1870s that a typewriting machine would be available in police stations. Reporters on local papers, hungry for stories, would haunt the magistrates' courts for newsworthy items, but it was not until the 1880s that the 'new journalism' turned to crime reporting to boost newspaper circulation and that coup was effectively the work of one man – Jack the Ripper.

Highgate had something of a Bohemian reputation in the Victorian period, which may account for the cross-dressing. Polite society had been appalled in the previous year when Ernest Boulton and Frederick Park were tried on a charge of 'conspiring and inciting persons to commit an unnatural offence'. They appeared in court wearing full female get-up.

Boulton wore a cherry-coloured evening silk dress trimmed with white lace ... he had on bracelets. He wore a wig and plaited chignon. Park's costume consisted of a dark green satin dress, low necked and trimmed with black lace ... His hair was flaxen and in curls.

While Superintendent Thomson of E Division and his men could splutter outrage all they liked, Boulton and Park had actually broken no laws by wearing female gear and since actual anal sex could not be proved (despite examination by the police surgeon) the two men walked.

If men posing as women was unusual – and outrageous – the reverse was so odd as to be remarkable. Arthur Munby, who had a fascination with working girls[4], records two instances in his diary. The first was in 1861 where Mary Newall appeared at Westminster Police Court accused of robbing her employer. What fascinated Munby was that she had done a runner to Yarmouth in men's clothes, smoked cigars and made love to the landlady of her lodging house. In 1867 Munby was at Southwark Police Court discovering that Thomas Walker, barman at a pub in the London Road, was actually a woman. 'Thomas' certainly looked the part, with short hair, brawny arms and a bull neck, but the crime she was charged with was theft from her employer. Munby had some sympathy for her, commenting 'the magistrate was pompous and petulant and grandiose, as one might expect ...'[5]

We have no details of the Abberline case, but again, the actual crime for which they would have been sentenced was disorderly conduct.

The year of 1867 was a momentous year for Frederick Abberline. The activities of the Irish republican Fenians in that year are chronicled in the next chapter, but watching and reporting on their activities meant that Abberline was in plain clothes for most of the year. It is possible to argue that this was detective work, the Detective Branch at Scotland Yard having been set up in 1842, but in reality Abberline had yet to take that career step. Plain clothes for policemen had been rejected in 1829 as smacking of a government spy network, but by 1833 the Police Orders said that each division was to provide two of 'their most active and intelligent men in plain clothes to apprehend thieves and pickpockets'[6]. A parliamentary select committee had no problem with that as long as order was maintained and criminals caught. It was not until 1868, however, (perhaps as a result of Fenian surveillance) that a clear division was made between detectives and 'uniform'. Indeed, plain-clothes duty, often called Winter Patrol, was carried out month by month, interspersed with uniformed patrols.

It is not entirely clear when Abberline eventually became a detective, but it was probably in 1871. It would be some time before a 'them and us' culture developed between detectives and 'uniform', but the inference was always that only the ablest policemen went on to the detective force, leaving the others to tell people the time and watch the horse troughs.

If there are hazy areas in the record of Abberline's career, his private life is almost a closed book. His sister Emily married James Rice in 1865 and they had three children; Ada, who was born in Lambeth two years later; Frederick (possibly named after his uncle) in Newington in 1873 and Henry, born in 1877. Frederick's elder brother Edward married Helen (or Ellen) McKay in 1871 and they too had three children; Helen, born at Farnham in the same year; Cora at Chatham two years later and Edward junior in 1875. The fact that the boy was born in Malta is a reminder that Edward was in the navy and the family were posted abroad with him.

On 5 March 1868, Frederick Abberline married, at St James's Church, Islington, Martha, the twenty-one-year-old daughter of labourer Thomas Mackness. We know nothing about this lady except that she probably hailed from Northamptonshire. Her birth is listed in the last quarter of 1847 at Oundle. How they met and what form their courtship took is unknown, but it is safe to say the Macknesses were probably living in Islington, because that is where the marriage took place. Since Abberline was a sergeant by then he *may* have been able to afford lodgings for himself and his wife. The Abberlines' wedding certificate lists their address as St James, Holloway.

But wedded bliss was not to last long. In May 1868 Martha Abberline died of consumption, the killer disease that was virtually endemic in London. Two years earlier a serious attack of cholera had hit the Islington/Highgate area, a harsh reminder of just how fragile life was in Victoria's England. But Martha died at Elton, Northamptonshire. John Wilson's *Imperial Gazetteer* of 1870–72 describes the village as standing 'on the verge of the county and on the river Nen'. The Northampton-Peterborough railway ran through it and it had a station and post office. The population stood at 947 and there were 211 houses, one of them quite probably belonging to one of the Mackness family. According to research carried out for the Jack the Ripper Forum, the Mackness family, led by Tobias, lived in Duck Street. In the 1861 census, Tobias was forty-three and his wife Frances forty. They had five children at that point; John was seventeen and a labourer like his father; Rebecca was two years younger with no occupation given; Martha was thirteen then and still at school; as was William, nine. The youngest child, Thomas, was only a month old.

Roblee, on behalf of the Forum, suggests that Martha went to London in search of work, leaving her family behind, and returned home when she became ill. This is a possibility, but because we have no idea of the Mackness family relationships, we cannot be sure. On the face of it, it seems unlikely that a young girl would simply pack her bags unless there was a relative or family friend already in London to give her support.

What we can be sure of is that the 1871 census records Abberline, now a widower, at Kentish Town Road police station, along with another eleven officers. It is often assumed that *all* these men were widowers. Even allowing for the high mortality rate, this seems very unlikely as their average age is twenty-two! The census itself makes it clear that Abberline was the only widower, the others being unmarried. Clearly the sergeant was back in a Section House again, but a new direction beckoned and he would make his name in 'the Abyss'.

Chapter 4

'Glory O! Glory O!'[1]

When Frederick Abberline was two and a half years old a blight hit the potato crop in Ireland, not once but three times. There was nothing new in this; in the century before 1841 there had been no fewer than seventeen failures, each one bringing misery, desperation and death. What was different about 1845 was the sheer unbelievable scale of the disease's spread.

In the early summer of that year, the crop looked exceptionally strong and healthy, but a sudden change in the weather, with weeks of torrential rain, told a different story. The blight itself came from America and turned the potatoes black, foul-smelling and squelchy in the ground – too rotten even to be dug.

On 13 September Dr John Lindley, editor of the *Gardeners' Chronicle and Horticultural Gazette* and Professor of Botany at the University of London, told the world:

> We stop the Press with very great regret to announce that the potato Murrain [disease] has unequivocally declared itself in Ireland. The crops about Dublin are suddenly perishing ... where will Ireland be in the event of a universal potato rot?[2]

The answer was: in a very serious situation indeed. Despite efforts by the British government under Robert Peel who sent wheat, Indian maize and cash to Ireland, it was too little, too late. Ireland had become hopelessly wedded to the potato – it was cheap to grow, required only basic agricultural skills and could feed people and animals alike. It could even – in the form of 'poteen' – provide a rot-gut alcoholic drink swigged from Donegal to Kerry.

The system of land tenure in Ireland, by which tenants sublet to sub-tenants in a vain attempt to afford the extortionate rents fixed by English, often absentee, landlords, was ideal for potato-growing but totally inadequate for wheat, oats and barley. And there was virtually no industry in Ireland to finance the technology necessary for the steam-driven machinery that was being introduced in England.

The results of the potato crop failure were disastrous, producing a human tragedy unparalleled in Western Europe. Just before Christmas 1846, the Cork magistrate Nicholas Cummins wrote to the Duke of Wellington, himself an Irishman, and sent a copy to *The Times*, then read by anybody who was anybody.

> In the first [sod-built hut in the village of Skibareen] six famished and ghastly skeletons, to all appearances dead, were huddled in a corner on some filthy straw, their sole covering what seemed to be a ragged horsecloth, their wretched legs hanging about, naked above the knees ... They were in fever, four children, a woman and what had once been a man ... in a few minutes I was surrounded by at least 200 such phantoms, such frightful spectres as no words can describe ... Their demoniac yells are still ringing in my ears ...

Whole villages vanished. Parish priests, overworked and helpless, officiated at mass burials. In the more remote areas, bodies were found by the roadside or in ditches, lying where they had fallen, too weak from hunger to move.

Accurate population figures are difficult to come by for Ireland. The 1841 census, which is the first one accepted by historians as plausible, gives a national figure of 8,175,124. Ten years later, when the famine had done its worst, it was 6,552,385. In the four provinces, Leinster lost 15.5% of its population; Ulster (the richest area) 16%; Munster lost 23.5% and Connaught, in the desperately poor west, 28.6%. Nearly 360,000 mud and turf hovels disappeared because there was no one to occupy them.

The Irish potato famine was not the cause of Anglo-Irish discontent. That had been a feature of British life since the twelfth century, when racial and religious divisions had been exacerbated by a chaotic and primitive agricultural system which created appalling poverty long before the blight hit. What the famine did, however, was to kick-start a nationalist movement that would, in the long run, see the creation of an independent Irish state and in the shorter term impacted on hundreds of British policemen like Frederick Abberline.

Approximately one million people died during the years of the famine and a further million emigrated, some, like Lord Palmerston's tenants, being given the £5 a head necessary to take them in cattle pens to America, Canada or Australia. An estimated 300,000 arrived in Liverpool and many of them drifted east to areas like Whitechapel and Spitalfields, where Abberline would spend nearly half his career as a detective. In some ways, luck was with these desperate emigrants. A gold strike in California in 1849 provided hope of untold riches; a smaller find in Australia two years later had a similar effect. And it was not just the illusion of a fortune which provided comfort for the escapers of the famine. The railway boom in Britain in the otherwise 'hungry forties' meant that work for navvies was plentiful. They built shanty towns near the track, with colourful names like Jericho and Batty Wife-Hole. They sold their shovels for cider and drank and fought their way across the country; but they built the network for which Britain was once famous. In the process, for nearly thirty years, they earned four times what a farm labourer could and, while the work was hard and dangerous, it must have represented paradise after the death of the 'praties' in rain-sodden Mayo.

Visitors to pre-famine Ireland often remarked on the cheerfulness of the inhabitants. The writer Walter Scott said in 1825 'their natural condition is turned towards gaiety and happiness.'[3] 'If there be a market to attend,' wrote George Nicholls, a Poor Law expert, 'a fair or a funeral, a horse race, a fight or a wedding, all else is neglected and forgotten.'[4] But what was not forgotten – or forgiven – was the centuries of oppression the Irish had suffered at the hands of English landlords and the famine was the last nail in the coffin of Anglo-Irish relations. Those who emigrated to America in particular carried their grievances with them and the infectious, national gaiety became morose, introverted, vengeful. The immediate post-famine situation in Ireland gave hope that William Smith O'Brien's Young Ireland movement could achieve something among Irish nationals convinced that all their problems should be laid at England's door. Smith O'Brien himself was not a revolutionary, but a series of revolutions sweeping across Europe in 1848 spoke of all sorts of possibilities in a brave new world.

'Then up with the barricades and invoke the god of battles,' wrote Thomas Meagher, another Young Irelander in the organization's newspaper *The United Irishman*. He advocated guerrilla warfare, throwing flowerpots, furniture, pokers and chamber pots at the English troops stationed on Dublin's streets. English cavalry were to be hampered by showers of broken glass which would cripple their horses; infantry were to be lured down alleyways to be hit by boiling water and flying grease. Meagher and O'Brien hoped for defections too – a third of the British army was composed of Irishmen. In the event, the Young Ireland rebellion was a joke. There were possibly as many as eighty revolutionary clubs in Ireland during the Year of Revolutions, but they were totally uncoordinated and often refused to cooperate with each other. O'Brien's vaunted 50,000 rebels had dwindled to fifty by July and he wept 'silent tears of shame and despair'.

But out of the failure of Young Ireland emerged a far more determined and organized opposition – the Fenian Brotherhood. The movement took its name from the Fianna, legendary Irish heroes of the second and third centuries led by the mythical Fionn mac Cumhail. It claimed that many of its ideas went back to the United Irishmen organization of Wolfe Tone in the 1790s, but the founders of the Fenians in 1858 were James Stephens, John O'Mahoney, Michael Doheny and John Dillon. All four had escaped to Paris to avoid prosecution in English courts and while O'Mahoney set up the Fenians in America, Stephens returned to Ireland and founded the Irish Republican Brotherhood on St Patrick's Day.

From the outset the Fenian movement, whichever side of the Atlantic, had one aim – Irish independence. And it was prepared to use violence to achieve it. It was a secret society and found itself at odds with the Irish Catholic clergy and most ordinary peasants. Neither did it find favour with other radical organizations, especially when 1867 brought outbreaks of violence which were seen by most people as a step too far. The infant trade union movement shunned the Fenians; so did the Reform League. Charles Bradlaugh, the radical MP who could usually be counted on to take on any crusade, wrote in his *National Reformer* that the events of 1867 were 'calculated to destroy all sympathy and to evoke the opposition of all classes'. Karl Marx, then in London and working steadily towards the Utopia he believed would be created by a revolution of the proletariat, wrote to a friend: 'The London masses, who have shown great sympathy towards Ireland, will be made wild and driven into the arms of a reactionary government.'

In his retirement speech from Scotland Yard in May 1892, Frederick Abberline recounted that he spent twelve months in 1867 in plain clothes, even though he was not yet technically a detective. What was happening in those months and why was it all so secret?

The plan for revolution was prepared by Thomas Kelly, who styled himself 'Colonel' and 'Deputy Central Organiser of the Irish Republic'. Kelly, like several other rebels of 1867, had served in the Union Army in the American Civil War, so he understood tactics and was hardened to violent death.[5] He tried to seize the arsenal at Chester Castle and failed, turning his attention instead to fund-raising and gaining support. He wrote: 'We intend no war against the people of England; our war is against the aristocratic locusts, whether English or Irish, who have eaten the verdure of our fields.'

On 11 September Kelly and co-rebel Timothy Deasy were found loitering by police in Oak Street in the Shudehill district of Manchester and were challenged under the Vagrancy Act. Once it was known who the two were, the police presence around them multiplied and they were taken to Belle Vue gaol under heavy guard. There were four other prisoners in the horse-drawn van, but the only officer inside with them was Sergeant Charles Brett, armed with a cutlass.

At the point where a railway arch crossed the Hyde Road, a group of Fenians came out of nowhere and shot the horses. They hammered the van with hatchets, sledgehammers and crowbars in an attempt to free their leaders, but nothing worked until one of them blew off the lock with his pistol. Unfortunately, Sergeant Brett was peering through the keyhole at that moment and the ball smashed through his eye-socket, killing him instantly. Brett was the first Manchester policeman to be killed in the line of duty; he was fifty-two. Kelly and Deasey had urged him to hand over the keys seconds before he died, but he said, 'I dare not; I must do my duty.' The words were carved on his gravestone and the memorial to him in

St Barnabas Church, Ancoats, called him 'a victim of the violence of sedition'.

If Kelly and Deasy got away to America, others involved did not. Twenty-six Fenians squeezed somehow into the dock. Their fates varied; some turning Queen's evidence against the others; some serving years in the New Bailey Gaol in Salford. Three were hanged; William Allen, a carpenter from Cork who may have actually pulled the fatal trigger; Michael O'Brien, an Irish American who had served in Kelly's regiment in the Civil War; and Michael Larkin, a tailor, described as a hapless victim of men like O'Brien. Allen made a fiery Republican speech in his own defence. O'Brien, as an American citizen, tried to get the United States government involved, but they turned their backs.

The 'Manchester Three' were doubly unfortunate in that their executioner was the bungling William Calcraft. Death threats were made against him and he was glad to leave the city once his job was done. They instantly became martyrs, a fiction that has lasted in Manchester to the present day, and there were demonstrations of protest about the hanging in Liverpool, Sheffield and Birmingham. It was the events in London, of course, that involved Frederick Abberline.

Clerkenwell had a reputation for radicalism long before 1867. Earlier in the century it had seen rallies and demonstrations by dispossessed men, desperate for a better deal in life and hoping for the vote. Spa Fields in nearby Islington was the setting for a vast public meeting in 1816 when the authorities feared revolution and the army was on standby. When news of the Fenian hangings became common knowledge, a 2,000-strong demonstration, mostly of Irish males, gathered broodingly on Clerkenwell Green. They carried banners that read 'Man's inhumanity to man makes thousands mourn' and the whole thing was more a show of sorrow than of anger. Fifes and drums played solemn music and there was no trouble.

Abberline had been promoted sergeant in Y Division two years earlier. He was still stationed in Highgate, but in 1867 men from Divisions were drafted in to different areas as they would be to Whitechapel twenty-one years later during the Ripper scare. There was a sense of fragility in the Met in the late 1860s. Thousands gathered in Hyde Park to demand the extension of the vote, as promised to them by William Gladstone and the Liberals. Alarmed at the potential for disturbance, the Home Secretary, Spencer Walpole, banned public meetings, thereby exacerbating an already tense situation. Some 3,200 policemen were drafted in and the aged Commissioner, Sir Richard Mayne, personally led them on horse-back. While the legitimate Reform League supporters gave way and listened peacefully to a speech from the firebrand MP John Bright, the mob that always accompanies such meetings stayed in Hyde Park to tear down the railings and fight the police. Mayne was hurt and twenty-eight officers injured for life. The Guards were called in, the first time since the creation of the Met that the army had been sent for 'to aid the civil power'. It was the first of many 'bloody Sundays' and Mayne became the focus of blame, as always carrying the can for politicians.

It may have been no more than coincidence that Fenian activity moved to London a few months later and central to it was another ex-Civil War soldier, 'Colonel' Richard O'Sullivan Burke. He was in the capital in November visiting the Irish contingent in their heartlands of Whitechapel and Spitalfields. Although most of them lived in the worst conditions, some of them were 'respectable' with jobs such as porters, carmen and dock labourers. A few owned ale and chop houses. After 1846, however, the huge influx of famine survivors changed that and, effectively denied help from the New Poor Law, Irishmen were constantly before the courts on various vagrancy charges.

Burke was a wanted man and was arrested at gunpoint in Woburn Square, Bloomsbury, in the middle of November, ending up in Clerkenwell gaol. Letters written in invisible ink were passed to Burke from his sister via his solicitor and by that means a plot was hatched to break him out using dynamite. On 12 October two labourers, trying to look as casual as possible, rolled a cart with a barrel of gunpowder in it against the prison wall, lit the fuse and ran. Nothing. The powder failed to ignite.

British intelligence, working out of Dublin Castle and led by Robert Anderson, who would one day become Abberline's ultimate boss at the Yard, had enough information to sound a warning and Burke was moved to the far side of the prison. The next day, unaware that the game was up, three men rolled a tarpaulin-covered barrel cart along Corporation Lane, even having the audacity (or stupidity) to ask a child the way to the gaol. This time the fuse worked and the resulting explosion blew out the prison wall and all but demolished 39 Corporation Lane, which was only eight yards from the gaol itself. Other houses in the street rattled and windows shook. The result was twelve dead and over forty wounded. A horrified Press claimed that twenty babies had 'died in the womb'.

Burke was still secure, but the comments by Bradlaugh and Marx quoted above make it quite clear that Clerkenwell had an adverse effect and the terrorism of the Fenians appalled all elements of Victorian society. Richard Mayne estimated there were some 10,000 armed Fenians in London and, assuming Clerkenwell to be the start of a major campaign, had 50,000 special constables sworn in. In something of a panic, government officials had their office floors covered in sawdust in an attempt to combat the effects of the dreaded 'Fenian Fire' (a sort of napalm) which was, along with dynamite, the 'new'[6] secret weapon of the Irish Republicans. There were dozens of arrests, but most of the cases collapsed through lack of evidence and only Michael Barrett faced the rope. Like Allen he made an impassioned political speech from the dock, but the mood of London had changed and no one made a martyr out of Michael Barrett. He appears as a footnote in history, however, as the last man to die on a public gallows; after his, all executions were carried out within prison walls. Calcraft was unusually efficient outside Newgate that day, but so unpopular was the man that, when he came back to check on Barrett's body the routine hour after hanging, someone in the crowd yelled 'Come on, bodysnatcher'.

Many were furious that so many Fenians had escaped. Queen Victoria, still the reclusive 'Widow at Windsor' after the death of her beloved Albert, suggested suspending habeas corpus and wrote to the Home Secretary, Gathorne Hardy, '. . . one begins to wish those Fenians would be lynch-lawed on the spot.'[7]

Abberline's precise role against the Fenians is unknown. His retirement reminiscences included a jovial memory of mixing with Fenians at a ball, which seems unlikely. Did the Dorsetman go undercover to monitor Fenian activities in London? Only, I suspect, if he could do the accent. An Irishman would naturally be suspicious of an over-friendly Englishman and his cover would soon be blown. The Met was divided over the use of disguises but they were used to good effect both before and after the creation of the Detective Branch in 1842. The famous photograph of Limehouse CID in 1911 shows men with over-the-top hooks for hands, missing arms and eye-patches, and surely could have fooled no one. On the other hand, Chief Inspector John Littlechild, whose career in some ways parallels Abberline's, wrote in his reminiscences: 'but let a detective put on, I will say, a butcher's smock, apron and a steel and who shall recognize him in his get-up?' He himself occasionally played surveyors and sanitary inspectors!

What is certain is that Abberline was caught up in the fall-out from Clerkenwell, which affected the whole of the Met. The Home Secretary formed a counter-revolutionary secret service department under Colonel William Fielding with Adolphus 'Dolly' Williamson and James Thomson seconded to it from Scotland Yard. Williamson was a no-nonsense copper of the old school, having joined the Met in 1850. By the time of Clerkenwell he was an inspector, as popular with the rank and file as he was with his superiors. He was a noted practical joker, no mean singer and kept fit by rowing on the Thames. Much of his time in the late 1860s was taken up with watching the Fenians so he was a natural for Fielding's unit. The civilian secretary was Robert Anderson, with his inside knowledge of Irish problems gleaned from his time at Dublin Castle. As with many police initiatives before and since, budgets played their part and once the Fenian scare died down, Fielding's unit was disbanded. It is unlikely that Abberline was actually part of this group, although it is not impossible and would certainly explain his being in plain clothes for so long – the unit lasted for five months.

What Manchester and Clerkenwell did was to galvanize the government into action. The new Prime Minister in 1868, William Gladstone, famously told the Commons – and everybody else – that it was his 'mission ... to pacify Ireland' and to that end he pushed through two acts of parliament to solve the 'Irish question', as the on-going situation became known. As a deeply religious man, Gladstone passed the Irish Church Act, disestablishing what was a Protestant church in a largely Catholic country, and he followed this up with a Land Act that was designed to protect the tenant from the avarice of the landlord. In fact this was badly constructed and the dreaded power of eviction which landlords held over their tenants continued.

Fast forward to 1885. By this time, Frederick Abberline was local inspector, in charge of the CID in H Division, Whitechapel. He had been there for twelve years and enjoyed the work so much he had already turned down the offer of a post at Scotland Yard because it would have meant leaving the area.

The 1870s had been largely quiet in terms of Anglo-Irish relations while men waited to see what the effects of Gladstone's Acts would be. Even so, in Ireland itself, the one-armed Fenian Michael Davitt formed the Irish Land League. He had been released early from a fifteen-year prison sentence and with American money set up a socialistic group in 1879 to fight for tenants' rights. Far more dangerous from the London establishment's point of view was Charles Stewart Parnell. With his moneyed background, his Cambridge education and his determination to establish Home Rule for Ireland, he went head to head with the British government, advocating the 'boycotting'[8] of English landlords and introducing filibustering, whereby the Irish MPs at Westminster used delaying tactics to fill the tight parliamentary schedule with Irish issues. A commission was held in 1887 to inquire into Parnell's links with the Fenians, but they had already struck without him.

Bombing campaigns began again in 1881 with Liverpool, Glasgow and London being the major targets. As with later outrages by the IRA, there is some doubt as to whether the actual targets were people or buildings, but the indiscriminate risk to life was what appalled the legal establishment and society generally. It was only the unpredictable nature of dynamite and fuses that meant that the number of deaths was so low. In March 1881 a bomb was defused at the Mansion House, the headquarters of the mayor of London. The following year one exploded, but there was no loss of life. In March 1883 two bombs went off in Whitehall and at the offices of *The Times* newspaper, and on 30 October the underground system was first hit. Praed Street and Westminster Bridge stations were the first casualties and seventy people were injured. The following

February dynamite was left in the left luggage office at Victoria Station, but the building itself was empty and no one was hurt.

From that point on, however, the Fenian campaign was stepped up. On 30 May 1884 a bomb exploded at Scotland Yard, possibly aimed at 'Dolly' Williamson's Special Irish Branch that had been formed a year earlier. The man operationally in charge here was Inspector John Littlechild and the unit had received an anonymous letter threatening to 'blow Superintendent Williamson off his stool'. According to that note every public building in London was a potential target, but perhaps no one believed the Fenians would have the nerve to carry out a direct attack and that the threat was literal. Again, the building was empty when the bomb went off just before 9.00pm, but those living nearby and a passing cabman were hit by flying glass. The bomb had been placed in a cast-iron urinal and the corner of the building was blown away, leaving a hole 30 feet by 15 feet. Williams's office was a shambles and photographs taken the next morning show the precincts full of debris and the windows of the Rising Sun pub opposite blown out.

But the Yard was only one target of that potentially deadly night. Another bomb went off in the basement of the junior Carlton Club, headquarters of the Conservative Party in Pall Mall. A second exploded outside the house of Sir Watkin Williams-Wynn, the Welsh Conservative MP for Denbighshire, where ten people were injured. And it was perhaps only luck that the bomb placed at the foot of Nelson's Column in Trafalgar Square was found and defused. The column, to one of England's greatest heroes[9], was 169 feet tall and could have done untold damage.

The British public might have breathed a sigh of relief and had a sense of poetic justice when three members of the IRB were killed while planting a bomb at London Bridge on 13 December 1884, but this was merely a technical hitch in the 'dynamite war' and further plans were afoot.

James Gilbert Cunningham, who often used his middle name as an alias, was twenty-two. He was short, muscular, clean shaven and, according to newspaper reports of the time, 'unmistakenly Irish type'. His eyes twinkled. He had dark curly hair and an upturned, almost comical nose. Self-possessed and assured, the Irishman landed at Liverpool on 20 December 1884 on board *The Atlantic* and stayed at Stock's Hotel for three days. In common with many assiduous hoteliers, John Stock or one of his people hung around the docks touting for custom and Cunningham had accepted his offer. From there, Cunningham caught a train to London and was seen with a large American trunk. A particularly observant railway porter, William Brookes of the Northern London Railway at Broad Street station, remembered the trunk was heavy and it slipped in being loaded. That was on Christmas Eve.

Mrs Winifred Cannon of 30 Great Prescott Street, Whitechapel, noticed that when Cunningham arrived looking for lodgings, he had no luggage with him, but when he returned later he was hauling a trunk. The new lodger called himself Gilbert and took a front bedroom on the third floor at a rent of five shillings a week. He told her he was a travelling salesman from Liverpool and stayed for seven days. He made no complaints, behaved normally, often visited the Catholic church next door and left abruptly without saying goodbye.

From there, Cunningham turned up at the door of Mrs Sarah Moore of 32 Scarborough Street, two streets away from Mrs Cannon's. He told Mrs Moore that his previous lodgings had not suited him because his bedroom was not arranged properly. By way of small talk, she asked him if he were a tailor or a Jew (did she have an antipathy to either of those?) and he told her he was not currently employed but was 'looking for a situation'. He paid a week's rent in advance (again, five shillings for a first floor ante-room) and gave the name of Dalton, an alias he had used before. That was bad luck for Cunningham because it was the name of Sarah Moore's relatives, and she mentioned it later when the police came calling. 'Dalton' was out most days between 9.00am and 6.00pm and occasionally in the evenings too. He always locked his room, but left the key hanging outside so that Mrs Moore could clean it.

Harry Burton was slight, with brown hair, a fair moustache, a long, aquiline nose and sunken cheeks. A cabinet maker by trade, he had reached Liverpool on Christmas Eve aboard the *Oregon* and this was not his first visit. The previous February, using the name of Edward Bolton, he had sailed from New York on a German ship, the *Donau*, with other Irish Americans. At Southampton he had bought a portmanteau which he packed with cakes of Atlas Powder A, a particular brand of ligneous dynamite made in a Philadelphia chemical works and fitted with several detonators in case one should fail to go off. The plan then had been to hit four railway stations – Victoria, Ludgate, Paddington and Charing Cross. In the event, only the Victoria bomb went off, in the station cloakroom on 25 February. The timing was wrongly set on the Paddington fuse and the bomb effectively dismantled before it exploded. At Ludgate a pistol was used to ignite the case but the cartridge failed to explode, and at Charing Cross Burton's case was found containing a newspaper dated 21 February. The case had been left there that day between 6.00 and 7.00pm and it also contained a frock coat with unusual buttons that witnesses later remembered Burton wearing.

The 25th was the day that Burton probably left London for his own safety, but he was back by 16 May working for Hermann's factory in the East End. There was little doubt that Burton certainly, and Cunningham probably, were involved in all the explosions of the 'winter campaign' between 1883 and 1885.

On 12 January 1885 Burton turned up at the cab rank in Aldgate and hired Robert Crosbie to collect a passenger and trunk from Great Prescott Street 'just past the Roman Catholic church'. It was a freezing night and Crosbie was concerned for his horse and cab on the icy side roads. The pair haggled and Crosbie eventually took the job for two shillings. It struck Crosbie as odd that his fare seemed to collect a trunk, not from the front door of any house, but from the pavement near some railings, as if it had been left there for him. Crosbie took his passenger and trunk to 90 Turner's Road, Bow. This was the lodging house run by Mrs Frances Harvey and Burton had been staying there for five days before he turned up with the American trunk, which he placed in his room. Burton seemed unwell during these days – although the cabman Crosbie recollected having a cheering nip in a pub in Limehouse with Burton during the journey to Bow. The only visitor Burton had at Turner's Road was a Mr Dietz, the foreman at Hermann's where Burton worked.

Saturday, 24 January 1885 became known as Dynamite Saturday. At 2.40pm that afternoon an urgent telegram came through to Inspector Abberline at the Commercial Road police station. A bomb had exploded at the Tower, which was on his patch. Hurtling to the

43

place in a Maria, Abberline found the gates locked and smoke drifting across Tower Hill, with crowds of astonished on-lookers craning their necks to get a better view. The constable on duty opened a side gate and let his guv'nor in.

The Tower of London was already a major tourist attraction by 1885 and there were over 200 people there that day, many of them Jews not taking Shabbos too seriously. When the bomb had gone off, quick-thinking PC Thomas Gallagher[10] had run to the main gates and locked them. This had taken him three minutes and in that time only a young couple with a baby had left. As the senior policeman now on the spot, Abberline must have been harangued by the 200, all of them terrified and desperate to get out. There was a shattered room in the banqueting hall of the White Tower, but who knew whether any other devices were still waiting to explode? In the event he made a brave decision, later backed by his boss, Superintendent Thomas Arnold, that no one was to leave and that his men would take statements from them all.

Abberline had been a policeman for twenty-two years by this time, a detective for fourteen. He prided himself on an understanding of what today we call body language and knew a villain at a hundred yards. And at some time during that cold, tense afternoon, while the tourists grumbled and the Yeomen of the Guard kept careful watch, he sat in the ticket office, facing one such villain. The man said he was James George Gilbert. He was an English labourer living at Cherbourg Street, Whitechapel. He'd only just arrived having worked for two to three weeks in Liverpool docks. He'd come to London to better himself. Abberline noted the Irish-American accent and told 'Gilbert' flatly he'd never heard of Cherbourg Street. The Irishman then corrected himself and gave the addresses in Prescott and Scarborough Streets. Abberline also noted that 'Gilbert' was very hesitant in his replies, usually repeating Abberline's questions, presumably to give himself time to think. The inspector searched his man and took three keys from him before passing him on to other officers to repeat the process. This was probably a time-honoured police ploy. Get the man rattled, get him to repeat his story, look for mistakes, inconsistencies. Nothing about 'Gilbert's' story added up.

Abberline visited the bomb site before the interrogations began. The device had been hidden behind a radiator which was itself screened by a stand of armour and muskets.[11] There was a gaping hole in the floor, weapons and debris everywhere. The injured were patched up and as soon as their details were taken, they were taken to the London hospital in Whitechapel High Street.

One of the injured was Annie Nunn, who had been visiting with her friend Elizabeth Bailey. They had just entered the banqueting hall when she had seen smoke rising from the right-hand wall and heard a 'dreadful noise' as the blast blew her backwards. She spent a week in hospital. Ernest Stratton, 'a sharp little lad' had gone to the Tower with his friend Herbert George. All he saw in the banqueting hall were the Beefeaters – Yeoman Warders – and a policeman. Then he smelt something 'like fusees' (fireworks) and the bomb went off. He got off lightly, but Ernest was hit by flying debris in the head, thigh and right hand. Abberline was increasingly convinced that 'Gilbert' was the bomber. He took him and his bags to 32 Scarborough Street and unlocked the trunk in his presence. This and a black portmanteau were taken away as evidence to Leman Street police station and 'Gilbert' was remanded in custody.

Burton had not been at the Tower that day. He had been busy planting a bomb at the House of Commons. Over a century of Irish terrorism has taught the British establishment to be wary and high-tech security systems today would make attacks like Cunningham's and Burton's virtually impossible. Key witnesses with good memories played into police hands, however, and Burton was arrested later that day.

Three days later the pair ('Gilbert's' real name was now known) were indicted at Bow Street magistrates' court. 'Dolly' Williamson watched on behalf of the Yard, as was customary, and Cunningham was led in surrounded by a posse of policemen and gaolers. He answered his name and spent most of the time drumming with his fingers on the Bow Street woodwork. Abberline was the only witness called and Cunningham watched the man he called 'the constable' very closely during the proceedings. He was remanded until the following Monday. So, too, was Burton.

The trial of the Dynamitards was one of the defining moments of Abberline's career and stopped the bombing campaign, at least for a while, dead in its tracks. Cunningham and Burton were charged under the Treason Felony Act, passed in the eleventh year of Victoria's reign. Of course, had any of the injured died, the charge would have been murder and the Irishmen would have faced the drop. There were nine technical counts against them and they were charged with attempting to 'deprive the queen and her imperial crown and by force to compel the queen to alter her policy and to upset the constitution of the country'. They were also charged under the Explosives Act, the 'dishonest or criminal use' of gunpowder. Clearly the prosecution, led by Mr Poland the Attorney General and one of the leading advocates of his day, had enough on these two to link them with the bombings at the Tower, the Carlton, the House of Commons and the attack on Wynn-Watkins in St James's Square. The proceedings lasted eight days (very long for a Victorian trial) and 110 witnesses filed into the box at the Old Bailey.

Abberline duly gave his testimony and was able to link Cunningham with the trunk which contained detonators and wrappings of Atlas Powder A. The inspector was exhausted. Not only was he coordinating the work of the H Division detectives, sifting the countless witness statements and depositions, often until four or five in the morning, but he was also having to report to Sir William Harcourt, the Home Secretary, every morning in his Whitehall offices. Harcourt was paranoid about Irish dynamite and with good reason, but it wore Abberline out.

For the defence Mr Richards, a relatively inexperienced barrister, tried the race card. Such was the hatred of Irish Americans since Clerkenwell, that he claimed that anyone with that background was a natural victim. He hoped 'it would not go forth to the sister isle [Ireland] and to the world that a man would not have a fair trial because he was an Irish American.' The police had behaved badly, using circumstantial evidence only. Cunningham had openly accused Abberline of planting a detonator in his trunk, even though Abberline didn't know one end of a detonator from another, never mind how to get hold of one. The only person who had seen Burton and Cunningham together was a Constable Roper and clearly he was mistaken, the defence alleged. As for the earlier railway bombings, on 2 January, two young ladies had given Cunningham an alibi for that evening and had 'no conceivable motive to speak untruths'. Since one of the girls was named O'Brien, the judge, prosecution and jury must have sat in astonishment at that remark!

When Poland made his closing speech for the prosecution, the writing was on the wall. He agreed that the simultaneous explosions of 1884, at the stations, could not have been the work of one man and regretted the fact that only Cunningham and Burton were in the dock. Poland blew great holes in the testimony of both men, reiterated PC Roper's statement that he had seen the pair eating in the Aldgate Restaurant together and answered Richard's defence pleas one by one. How did an out-of-work cabinet maker support himself and still be able to sail from America, pay his rent and buy expensive luggage? The answer was clear – he was a paid provocateur with money in his pocket from the Irish Republican Brotherhood. The whole business of changing addresses was to keep on the move and the trunk episode was necessary because a total of 80lbs of explosive had somehow to be passed between the pair so that their different targets could be hit.

Why hadn't Cunningham left the Tower before the bomb had gone off? Something must have gone wrong with the timing and, when it did, the Irishman found himself on the wrong end of an interrogation by Abberline, with ill-prepared answers and a flimsy story.

Mr Justice Hawkins, known as 'hanging Hawkins' in the gallows humour of the courts, summed up the following Monday. The crime, he said, was of 'diabolical character' and he urged the jury to be absolutely sure that the case against Cunningham and Burton was fully proved. They decided it was and it took them only fifteen minutes to do so.

Cunningham, speaking before sentence in a thick Irish accent said: 'I defy any man in the universe to prove me to be the cause of any explosion in London or any part of England whatsoever.' The police he said had been very kind, offering him whiskey and brandy. He thanked his friends – although he actually had none in England – and was ready to go to prison for life 'since my soul cannot be hurt'.

Burton, in a weak, feeble voice said: 'One day we shall all stand before the bar where justice is done and I hope all within my hearing will obtain more favourable judgement than I have from you.' The only proof against him was the prejudice of the English: 'Gentlemen, I am very proud to meet such a crowd of enthusiastic friends in the city of London.'

Hawkins was unimpressed and sentenced them both to 'penal servitude for the rest of your natural lives.'

'The utmost credit,' wrote *The Times* on 30 March, 'is due to the Metropolitan Police for the care with which the evidence has been collected and the indefatigable pains with which every clue has been followed up.'

Abberline and his fellow officers were officially commended by the judge and jury – one of eighty-four commendations the man would notch up before he left the Met – and Sir William Harcourt personally ordered that Abberline should receive £20 reward for his services.

No doubt, after the dust had settled, Frederick Abberline went home for a well-deserved sleep.

Chapter 5

The Abyss

To some it was the City of Dreadful Night; to others the Ghetto. To American journalist Jack London it was the Abyss, literally Hell itself. Nearly 500,000 people were crowded into the narrow, scum-cobbled streets of Whitechapel and Spitalfields. 'I should not like to hear them all talk at once,' London wrote in 1903. 'I wonder if God hears them?'[1]

The White chapel was probably the church of St Mary Matfelon, built in the fields outside the medieval city wall. And because the area was not subject to the City's bye-laws, Huguenot weavers, driven out from Catholic France by the revocation of the Edict of Nantes in 1689, settled in the place with their prosperity and their jacquard looms. By 1700 there were five Huguenot churches there with names like L'Hôpital, La Patente and Du Marché. The large, opulent weavers' houses, with their roof-level windows to let in as much daylight as possible, are still there along Church Street and Wilkes Street. Eighteenth-century prints show a wide High Street with elegant carriages and well-dressed citizens. By Abberline's time it was a slum, easily the worst in London.

The rot began with the fallout from the Irish potato famine. Over 300,000 men, women and children travelled east in a desperate escape to survival. Many got no further than Liverpool and Manchester; thousands of men became 'navvies', building the revolutionary railway network that was snaking across the land in the 1840s. Others got to London's East End and stayed. The Irish connection was still there in Abberline's time, apart from the work of the Dynamitards. Ripper victim Mary Kelly almost certainly came from Limerick. Thomas Conway, the husband of Kate Eddowes, also used the name Thomas Quinn and had served in the 18th Royal Irish Foot.

And as the Irish moved in so the Flemings, Walloons, Dutchmen and Frenchmen moved out. The Irish reputation for drinking, fighting and whoring was visited with a vengeance on the area that coincided with the Met's H Division and the police had a tough time of it. Their problems were exacerbated by the huge influx, after 1881, of Eastern European Jews.

The Jews had been driven out of medieval England by Edward I in 1290 and were not seen again until the 1650s when the oddly tolerant Puritan Oliver Cromwell let the Sephardic Jews return. Many of these were clothiers and tailors and set up prosperous businesses along the edge of what had once been Henry VIII's Artillery Ground. The Ashkenazi Jews followed and in the broadly liberal atmosphere of the laissez faire eighteenth century got along well enough with the Huguenots.

But all that would change in the 1880s because of sheer numbers. On 1 March 1881 the 'Tsar Liberator', Alexander II, had his legs all but blown off by the revolutionaries of The People's Will. His son, the no-nonsense Alexander III, who succeeded him the same day, ordered swift reprisals against dissidents throughout his vast empire. The Russian government had always been anti-Semitic and the Jews felt the full force of the pogroms. They fled their towns and villages and came west, to the greatest docks in the world in London, and moved just a few hundred yards to the cluster of tangled streets around Nicholas Hawksmoor's Christ's Church. They set up sweatshops, too small to be hassled by government legislation, and made and sold clothes at the Rag Fair. Chapels became synagogues, Shabbas became the holy day and the only Sunday street market in the country was set up along Wentworth and Middlesex Streets; it kept its sixteenth-century name – Petticoat Lane.

'But 'ow about this 'ere cheap immigration?' a Cockney asked Jack London when he was living in the area researching for his book. 'The Jews of Whitechapel, say, a-cutting our throats right along?'[2] It is against this racially tense background that we should see Charles Warren's decision to obliterate the infamous Goulston Street graffito – 'The Juwes Are Not the Men Who Will be Blamed For Nothing.' The last thing the Met wanted was wholesale anti-Jewish riots on their hands.

The Jewish influx led to impossible overcrowding, letting and sub-letting of properties for which landlords took rent but no respon-sibility. Jack London reported a family in St George's-in-the-East, in whose mortuary Ripper victim Liz Stride would be autopsied, living in a single room. Apart from the parents there were eight children, ranging in age from two to twenty. London divided the people of the Abyss into two – the employed and the down and outs. Street directories of the period list the first group – in Berner Street, where Liz Stride had her throat cut, Edwin Sumner was a greengrocer, John Sinkins was a chemist, Louis Hagens ran an off-licence and Louis Friedman baked unleavened bread. Crispin Street was home to farriers, basket makers, sack makers and saddlers. Isaac Mendoza sold furniture, Myers Markos made tinplate toys. London felt sorry for the 'full-bellied artisans at the doors' but he felt sorrier still for the others and was never the same after his experiences among them.

Poverty bred vice and drunkenness. The whole area was full of pubs and liquor sellers. Every one of the Ripper's victims had what today we call a drink problem. Despite Gladstone's licensing laws, brought in just before Abberline got to Whitechapel, cheap gin and beer were available round the clock and it was nonsense of the station sergeant to let Ripper victim Kate Eddowes out into the night of her death because it was too late to get more drink. The filthy streets may have been thick with a layer of grease, but they were never empty. Drunks and prostitutes roamed the alleyways at all hours and coster-mongers, dock labourers and warehousemen were up at three in the morning to start work at four. Everybody in the East End walked.

'Children are begotten in drunkenness,' wrote the journalist Edwin Pugh, 'saturated in drink before they drew their first breath, born to the smell and taste of it and brought up in the midst of it.'[3]

The reformer Frederick Charrington took up a personal anti-drink crusade after he saw a man kicking his wife on the pavement outside an East End pub that sold his family's beer. At that point, he threw away a fortune and campaigned to end the drunkenness and violence of the place. It did not work. Twenty years later Jack London wrote of the desperately poor:

To pound one's wife to a jelly and break a few of her ribs is a trivial offence compared with sleeping out under the naked stars because one has not the price of a doss. They become indecent and bestial. When they kill, they kill with their hands ... They gouge a mate with a dull knife ... They wear remarkable boots of brass and iron and when they have polished off the mother of their children with a black eye ... they knock her down and proceed to trample her ...[4]

'Domestics' like this were the daily and nightly routine for the patrolling constables of H Division.

The 'price of a doss' was 4d. That bought a hard, narrow vermin-infested bed in a common lodging house, with which the Abyss was crammed. Of the Ripper's victims, only one, Mary Kelly, had her own room and her rent was weeks in arrears. All the others were out on the mean streets earning their doss money, only to spend it on the drink that beckoned on every corner.

Walking into this hell-hole must have made Islington and High-gate seem like a paradise to Frederick Abberline. On 10 March 1873 he was promoted to inspector and transferred to H Division. Originally the rank of inspector lay midway between super-intendent and sergeant, but by the late 1860s the size of the metrop-olis meant an increase in the numbers and complexity of the police themselves. Sir Edward Henderson, Commissioner in 1869, split the rank into two – 2nd class inspector (Abberline in 1873) attached to sub-divisions, and 1st class attached to divisions. The whole structure would be re-evaluated to an extent by the great scandal and shake-up of the Turf Fraud case in 1877. We do not know where Abberline was living for his first three years in Whitechapel, but it is unlikely that an inspector would opt for a Section House, despite Henderson's on-going attempt to improve them. His salary would mean that he could afford a relatively comfortable lodging in the East End, although he would never stray very far from the Division headquarters in Leman Street.

H Division extended for 1¼ miles and it was served by four police stations. Apart from the headquarters at 76 Leman Street and the Commercial Street site at No. 160, which became Abberline's home after 1876, there was a station at King David's Street, Shadwell, and another at Arbour Square, Stepney. Thomas Arnold, Superintendent at H Division, lived at No. 36 nearby. Abberline's role now was very

different. He was a detective, constantly in plain clothes and probably already looking like a bank manager, as Walter Dew described
him in 1888. He may have carried a cane – the rather sinister one
bequeathed to Bramshill Police College in Hampshire was presented to him by brother officers as a mark of their esteem for him in
1888 and may have been chosen to replace an earlier one. He almost
certainly still patrolled the streets from time to time, as he was to
do again during the Ripper case, but now cases came to him via
constables and desk-sergeants. And of course, along with promotion
came a forest of paperwork, all of it still written longhand and
stored in wooden boxes.

Before 1878 the list of Abberline's 'collars' is once again sketchy.
He was present at the inquest into the death of Jeremiah Macna-
mara, murdered by Robert Wright in April 1873. In September he
charged Thomas Ross with running a gaming house. Two months
later Philip Hyams found himself under the inspector's gaze for
stealing with violence. And Abberline had no compunction about
'fighting city hall' either – he charged the Great Eastern Railway
Company with obstructing a public thoroughfare in November. But
drunkenness and violence, the culture that appalled Frederick
Charrington and Jack London as well as every other visitor to the
Abyss, loomed largest. In December, Isabella Shipley was charged
with drunken assault. In February 1875 he arrested Joseph Tedman
for stabbing John Bates and later in the year he felt Thomas
Herbert's collar because he had assaulted a policeman. In May 1876
he was looking into the death of 'Curly Kate' of Baker's Row, almost
certainly a prostitute killing of the type which would horrify the
world in 1888.

But the late 1870s saw more personal changes in the life of
Frederick Abberline because in 1876 he married thirty-two-year-old
Emma Beament, the daughter of a merchant from Hoxton New
Town, Shoreditch. As with his first wife, we have no idea how they
met or what form their courtship took, but her family's higher status
(in comparison with the Macknesses) speaks volumes for a class
consciousness that was becoming, if anything, more marked under
the late Victorians. The wedding seems to have taken place in
Hendon and by 1881 the Abberlines were living at Commercial
Road police station along with Inspector James Bugby and his wife

Mary. Unlike Leman Street, this building still stands, although it has an extra (fourth) storey which the Abberlines would not have known. The couple were to have no children but lived in apparent happiness for the next fifty-three years. Their private lives remain a closed book.

In the year after the Abberlines' wedding a scandal rocked Scotland Yard to its foundations and the shockwaves must have been felt by every detective in the Met. There was serious money to be made on the 'sport of kings' and a wealthy Parisian, Madame de Goncourt, was anxious to cash in on it. Accordingly, she placed a £30,000 bet on a horse in an English race at the suggestion of 'turf accountants' Harry Benson and William Kurr. Unfortunately for Madame de Goncourt the whole thing was, in twentieth-century phraseology, a 'sting'. The pair had a fraudulent racing paper printed and claimed to be working on behalf of a punter who was so brilliant at picking winners that no bookie would take his bets. The idea was that overseas punters would bet and they paid a commission to him for his tips. The brilliant tipster did not exist, the races did not exist and neither did the Bank of London, but Madame de Goncourt did not know that.

By the time the lady realized her error, Benson was in Amsterdam, but he was arrested by the Dutch police. Chief Inspector Nathaniel Druscovitch was sent by Superintendent Adolphus 'Dolly' Williamson to bring him back, but Druscovitch, despite being multi-lingual, seems to have bungled it. In the event, Benson and Kurr were finally arrested by Detective Sergeant John Littlechild in Edinburgh. They were subsequently tried and convicted.

This opened a can of worms – Inspector John Meiklejohn and Chief Inspectors Clarke, Druscovitch and Palmer were all caught with their hands in the till. Druscovitch had been working for Benson for four years and that is why he had so many problems trying to arrest him. The 'trial of the detectives' riveted Victorian society at all levels. Clarke was acquitted after an impassioned plea from Williamson (whose own career began to slide from this time) but the others were sent to gaol for two years. Palmer ran a pub afterwards and Meiklejohn became a private detective. Druscovitch died soon after his release.

The upshot of the Turf Club Fraud was a radical shakeup of the Detective Branch. Originally created in the year before Abberline was born, the plain clothes force was at first only eight men strong. It was headed by an ex-Bow Street Runner, Inspector Nicholas Pearce, but only two of the original team would reach national prominence – Stephen Thornton and Jonathan Whicher. Thornton hunted down the Mannings for their murder of an ex-lover of Maria Manning in 1849 and Whicher became famous for failing to nail sixteen-year-old Constance Kent for the murder of her little brother Saville in 1863. Never truly deserving of his reputation, Whicher became the blueprint for Wilkie Collins's Sergeant Cuff in *The Moonstone*. From the year in which Abberline joined the Met, 'Dolly' Williamson effectively ran the detective branch and achieved noteworthy successes. As we have seen, Fenian activity from the late 1860s kept the detectives on their toes. Until 1869, the only detectives in the Met operated out of Scotland Yard, but Sir Edward Henderson appointed them in Divisions with higher pay and a clothing allowance of £5 a year to purchase 'mufti'.

The cohesion of the Yard detectives fell apart as a result of the 1877 scandal and opened the way for a brave new world as envisioned by Howard Vincent. This extraordinary young man (he was only twenty-eight at the time) had a background in the army, the law and journalism and sent a report on Continental police systems to the Home Office. On the strength of that, quite bizarrely, he was appointed Director of a Criminal Investigation Department (CID) modelled on the Parisian Sureté but still accountable under the British constitution, with its use of magistrates' warrants and the existence of habeas corpus[5]. Howard Vincent worked alongside the Commissioner, Edward Henderson, on this and the actual leader of the new detective unit was 'Dolly' Williamson, ensuring continuity without the taint of corruption. The Divisions now had their own permanent detectives, always in plain clothes, and they were run by talented officers who were known as local inspectors. Abberline was promoted to this position in the April of the same year so he was now running the CID in H division. All serious crime, as well as relatively minor infringements, came his way. It is worth remembering that, as in the Ripper case which was to test the Met to breaking point, every crime committed in the Abyss would have crossed Abberline's desk at some point.

One of the consequences, perhaps unforeseen, of Howard Vincent's system was that CID officers, with their comfortable civilian clothes and better pay and allowances, were seen as an elite and this inevitably caused friction within the force. For most of the time this was kept under wraps and the two police strikes that took place while Abberline was on the force – 1872 and 1890 – were essentially about pay and the right to form a trade union. As his time in H Division wore on, the satirical magazine *Toby* described Abberline as:

> a well known East Ender [to whom] scores of persons are indebted. He has a decent amount of curiosity and has been known to stop gentlemen at the most unholy times and places and enquire about their health and work – questions which are often settled by a magistrate, generally in Mr Abberline's favour.[6]

There is little doubt that Frederick Abberline was a modest man, but from 1879 he began collecting newspaper cuttings about his cases and kept them, no doubt for his own amusement. It would be many years before he was persuaded to compile this into any coherent form with the occasional explanatory note in his own handwriting. The original book lies in the Historic Collection of the Metropolitan Police and I quote from it extensively here for the first time. Fifty-five cases are dealt with, covering a wide range of crimes. A further twenty-seven have been identified by researcher Simon Wood for the Jack the Ripper Casebook Forum and there are another fourteen listed on the Old Bailey website, giving us a total of ninety-six in a thirteen-year period. We can assume that these were cases in which Abberline was directly involved, as investigator, arresting officer or court witness; there must have been others covered by his detectives which he read and rubber-stamped. Two cases ominously missing from the cuttings book are the Ripper murders and the Cleveland Street scandal, which I deal with in later chapters. Abberline almost certainly regarded these as failures and the reporting of them by the Press was not conducive to collecting cuttings. At one extreme both local and national newspapers were awash with articles on the Ripper and no one, despite 120 years of research, has yet chronicled all these. At the other extreme, because of the sensitive nature of the Cleveland Street affair, which involved titled gentlemen and errand boys, very few papers wrote anything about it. The editor of one that did found himself in gaol for libel.

In keeping with the national picture, the most common crime with which Abberline had to deal was theft. If we throw into the mix the more specialized felony of burglary, these individuals account for forty percent of the cases he handled during his time in H Division. For reasons of space I will give just one example of each crime from the Abyss.

Maria Wood of 30 Trinity Square, Tower Hill, was walking along Mansell Street at noon one Saturday, probably in 1879[7], when she saw a scuffle break out ahead of her. The incident happened at the entrance to Haydon Passage, off the Minories, and three men were beating seven bells out of an 'aged man' carrying a bag. The old man was Isaac Harvey, a messenger who lived in the Minories and on the day in question he was carrying £50 in gold and £25 in silver, having been to the bank on behalf of his employer John Owen. It is not clear whether it was Mrs Wood or the dazed and battered Isaac Harvey who went to the police, but someone gave such an accurate description of one of the attackers that Inspector Abberline knew just where to look. He arrested William James, a labourer of George Street, at a coffee shop in Brick Lane and took him into custody. We have to remember the risks that men like Abberline routinely took. There are cases in which he wisely took a couple of officers with him, but just as often he arrested dangerous men on his own, carrying, at best, a tipstaff. He may, of course, have used his cane to good effect.

At Worship Street magistrates' court, Mr Saunders remanded James for a week. Only Abberline appeared at this stage and the evidence he gave was enough to commit James to trial. The man had 'previous'; he had been sentenced in June 1869 to ten years for 'larceny from the person' at Coldbath Fields, one of London's grimmest prisons. He had also been charged, along with George Smith, who was already in custody, with stealing £33 from Benjamin Prior, manager of the American Light and Oil Company. Prior's case was very similar to Harvey's; Smith had attacked him with a life-preserver[8] along Three Colt Lane, Bethnal Green, and was no doubt surprised when Prior fought back. James was hanging around and Prior assumed he was an innocent passer-by. The manager shouted at him to fetch a policeman and James simply ran.

At their trial, both men were found guilty. James was sentenced to twelve years. Because Smith pleaded guilty, he was given only eighteen months, although that was with the dreaded hard labour and twenty lashes of the 'cat', a leather or rope whip with at least three thongs that was designed to cut the skin to pieces. The Common Serjeant praised Abberline for his work on both cases (even though the third man in the Minories attack was never found) and this constitutes one of eighty-four commendations he received throughout his career.

Charles Coaffee, aged twenty-seven, was a ticket writer. Findlay Wentworth-Bart, five years younger, was an optician. John Sheen, aged twenty, was a tailor working near Leicester Square. Agnes Ralph, aged twenty-seven, was a bread-basket maker. What did they all have in common? They were 'concerned together in burglariously entering' the house of the Reverend Philip Wickstead at No. 7 Regent's Park Villas in the early hours of 4 October (probably 1878). The vicar's wife, Emily, had been asleep when she was woken at about twenty past midnight by the sound of a window opening and a heavy thud. She crept out of bed to see a light coming from the study and the silhouettes of two men. Scurrying back upstairs, she woke her husband who dashed downstairs. He got a knife in his stomach for his courage and the burglars got away with a silk purse containing thirty foreign coins, some silver cutlery, an overcoat and an ornate Norwegian dagger.

The press report does not explain exactly what role Agnes Ralph played in this, nor precisely which two men had been surprised by the vicar. Neither does it tell us how Abberline knew where to look for the suspects. The other oddity about the case is that it took place well out of H Division's jurisdiction, although the arrest happened in Whitechapel. This time, Abberline took three stalwarts with him, aware that he was dealing with at least one highly dangerous criminal. Sergeant George Foster and Constable Marriott are merely names on H Division's roster, but Sergeant William Thick, known to the criminal underworld as 'Johnny Upright', is the second most famous policeman on the Ripper case after Abberline. He had joined the Met five years after the man from Blandford and had a high reputation. Frederick Wensley, a young copper in 1888 and later one of the 'big four' at Scotland Yard, believed Thick to be one of the finest policemen he had known. Walter Dew, who would make his own name on the Crippen case in 1910, described him as 'a holy terror to the local law-breakers'. It was with him that Jack London stayed when writing *The People of the Abyss* in 1902. He was certainly the sort of man Abberline would want at his back, because the three burglars, found loafing in a Whitechapel tap room, turned violent and pulled a knife. We can only imagine what really lay under the paper's bland 'they were taken charge of' and ended up in custody. A search of Coaffee's house turned up the tell-tale Norwegian dagger and Agnes Ralph's pockets contained the stolen silk purse.

At the Old Bailey it became apparent that Bart, Coaffee and Sheen all had earlier convictions and they were sentenced to ten years in prison. Agnes Ralph got eighteen months with hard labour.

The usual partner in crime for theft and burglary was receiving stolen goods. Unusual items, such as the Norwegian knife, could be recognized easily, so the job of the 'fence' was to move contraband out of the area quickly and perhaps, in the case of jewels and precious metals, to break them up or melt them down to avoid detection. In a newspaper article headed 'A Modern Fagin' in December 1878, Stephen McCarthy of 42 Flower and Dean Street 'feloniously received' a gold watch, worth £14, which belonged to George Manser, shipwright of Blakeney Street, St George's-in-the-East. An expensive item like that could not be missed, as Manser had a note of its serial number. It was the usual story – men like McCarthy had a notorious track record, having been guilty of receiving at Hammersmith, Bow Street, Marlborough Street and even as far away as Warwick between 1860 and 1865. He had spent nearly three years in prison as a result and a further seven between 1866 and 1873. It was hardly dazzling police work, but still an intelligent piece of deduction on Abberline's part to know where to find the man and the loot.

In accordance with a psychological ploy which the police still use, Abberline, Thick and Marriott crashed into 42 'Flowery Dean' at 3.00am on Sunday morning. Not surprisingly, McCarthy was in bed, but not only was he half dressed, but a silver watch and a cigar box containing Manser's watch were also under the covers along-side him. 'You surely have not come to disturb me and turn me over at this time of the morning?' an outraged McCarthy asked Abber-line. On his way to Leman Street, the 'fence' asked the inspector if he could hang on to some of the stolen money, also found in his room, to pay his legal costs.

At the trial at the Middlesex Sessions before Mr Prentice QC, McCarthy tried the sympathy card. He turned up in a wheelchair although he could walk perfectly well and refused to 'lag' the three thieves who had stolen Manser's watch as he would rather have his head cut off. He then got belligerent, assuring the court that the 'party who put me away' ought to be burned. Abberline, Thick and Marriott were warmly commended for their work after McCarthy was sent down for seven years with a further seven under police supervision, the equivalent of parole today.

In a working-class area like Whitechapel, white-collar crime was relatively rare, but Abberline's cuttings include five cases of fraud. The case of Walter Reeves is undated, but it is likely to have been in the 1880s because Abberline knew the man well, having arrested him before. Then, he had been renting a workshop in Camden Town, (in Y Division's patch) and receiving letters at an address in Camden Road with a number of aliases. In what must have been the Victorian equivalent of a 'stake out', Abberline watched him for four days before moving in with his warrant. The scam that Reeves pulled was a common one at the time. He bought a musical box worth £7 from a Mr Baker of Saffron Walden, Suffolk, and deposited part of the sum with a financial agent, Richard Maynard of Hackney Road. Baker duly sent the box but did not receive the money. Agents like Maynard advertised their quite legitimate businesses in maga-zines like *Exchange and Mart* and he was horrified to learn that Walter Reeves was also Henry Gilbert and Frank Jolley and Charles Deacock, buying but never paying for sewing machines and canaries along with the aforesaid musical box. Along with Reeves's false names went a string of false addresses and it was Abberline's astuteness that enabled him to nab the fraudster, who was sent down for seven years.

Counterfeiting was an even more specialist form of white-collar crime, known to the underworld as 'smashing'. The 'king of the smashers' was Michael Crawley and Abberline's arrest of the man gave the inspector another commendation. Acting on information received (the familiar police jargon lets us know that Abberline had his 'snouts' and 'narks') he and Sergeant Thick went to 29 Old Church Road, Stepney, at 7.30 one evening and surprised two couples – Crawley and his wife Mary Ann and Margaret and Frederick Collard. So surprised were they that when the detectives burst in they panicked and struggled, coins flying in all directions. Abberline and Thick overpowered them and hauled them along to Arbour Square police station. None of the cuttings refers to exactly how difficult prisoners were taken to the cells. The Met had eight Black Marias by the 1880s, but these were usually used to transport prisoners to and from court. It is likely that Abberline and Thick merely frogmarched the 'coiners' along the streets.

At the subsequent trial, it turned out that Crawley led a gang of professionals that numbered as many as twenty. John Cobley testified that he rented out his house at No. 29 to Crawley, who had given the name Thompson and said he was a stevedore. Mary Towers, a barmaid at the Red Lion in Balaam Street, Plaistow, had served Crawley on the evening of the 29th and realized that the shilling he paid with was 'bad'. It was a similar story at the Enterprise in Halifax Street, Mile End New Town and the Railway Tavern in Stepney. It was difficult to make charges against the Crawleys and the Collards stick, because coins passed through many hands in the course of a day. Obviously, the more examples that could be laid at their door, the more suspicious it became. The raid by Abberline was conclusive, however – he found metal, files, ladles, plaster of Paris, fine sand and metal tongs, all the tools of a coiner. He and Thick picked up fifty shilling pieces, all dated 1872, some finished and some still rough. All four had 'previous' (Margaret Collard had twice been sent to the women's prison in Westminster) and the Common Serjeant had no hesitation in giving the Crawleys seven years and the Collards eighteen and twenty months respectively, with hard labour.

In August 1878, the dock at the Worship Street police court was crammed with sixteen prisoners, all of them accused of illegal betting. The gaming laws of the country were complicated and restrictive – they would not be relaxed until the 1960s and the fact that the police took them seriously is evidenced by the fact that Abberline's boss, Superintendent Thomas Arnold of H Division, personally led a raid, including inspectors Abberline and Holder, to No. 4 Boar's Head Yard behind Aldgate Station East. The door was locked until they hammered on it and when it was finally opened by Girshon Hirschfield, Abberline arrested him on a charge of keeping a gambling house. An unseemly scuffle broke out, with cards, cash and furniture flying everywhere. Once order was restored, with the eleven gamblers in handcuffs, Arnold's team found eighteen packs of cards, a quantity of loose change and (in Hirschfield's pocket) a lottery ticket.

Twelve of the sixteen were clearly East European Jews and one of them, Goldberg, turned Queen's evidence and told the court that he often went to Boar's Head Yard, usually on a Sunday, and had lost £25 in three weeks. Hirschfield was fined £50 and his wife was discharged – even though she was in full knowledge of the den, it could not be proved that she actually played or gambled. The others were fined £5 each, but many of them – perhaps because they had lost too much money – opted for prison sentences instead.

One of the biggest threats to city life was fire; and although by 1888 most of London was brick built and the Great Fire of 1666 something of an urban myth, old fears died hard. Many Londoners would vividly remember the great fire of Tooley Street south of the river in the 1860s and although Abberline himself was not in London at the time, it might explain his handwritten note alongside a case that came up in October 1887, the last one before he was transferred to A Division:

> I may mention that I took a lot of trouble over [the investigation of] this fire. There had been several fires at Whiteley's previously but none after this one. Although the jury thought otherwise, I was of the opinion that the fire was caused by spontaneous combustion[9] as up to this time a lot of things were kept on the premises such as lamp black and other things of a combustible nature.[10]

Whiteley's had opened its first store in 1863 and by the 1880s had a large staff of employees living in dormitories along the lines of other companies like Cadbury's in Bourneville and the Unilever works in Liverpool. The fire which broke out on 6 August was so serious that news of it was taken up by the foreign Press. The *New York Times* reported that the premises had been completely gutted with a financial loss of up to £500,000. At the time of the article, four bodies had been found among the rubble and the intensity of the flames caused an explosion. While Mr Whiteley himself dashed back from Ostend to visit injured employees and firemen in hospital, he himself was convinced of foul play. This was the fifth fire in his premises in five years and bursts of flames had been seen by a huge crowd on three floors simultaneously. Whiteley was now unable to insure his property as a result and refused to accept that the whole thing was coincidence.

Abberline and his team questioned over 100 witnesses and got nowhere. Even the experts were baffled. Captain Shaw, the Fire Chief, could not understand either how the fire had started, or what had caused the collapse of a wall which killed the four employees. Colonel Majendie, the government's explosives inspector, was sure there was no explosion, despite eye-witness evidence. Two engineers, Charles Walker and Chatfield Clarke, thought heat expansion had probably led to the rupture of stone and brickwork.

Whiteley offered a reward of £2,000, saying that 'the detective who put his hand upon [the arsonist] would have made his reputation for life.' That was not to be Abberline. The coroner's court merely registered the unfortunate deaths and the case remained unsolved.

One of the most peculiar cases that Abberline handled – and there were three of them – was dog-stealing. They all followed a similar pattern and in November 1878, Walter Cox, a servant working for Mr Denniston of Stanhope Gardens, Kensington, lost a black and white collie. He placed an advert in various papers and, as a result, John Moull, a general dealer of Old Nicol Street, Bethnal Green, called at Stanhope Gardens saying he knew the whereabouts of the animal and arranged to meet Cox the next day at the Prince of Wales pub in Holywell Lane, Shoreditch. Moull wanted £5 as a reward for the dog and a further £1 for his trouble. In court, Moull asked Abberline how he knew it was him – 'a request that caused some laughter.' Abberline had put the man in a line-up/identity parade at Commercial Street police station and Cox had picked

Moull out at once. With two previous counts of dog-stealing, the general dealer of Old Nichol Street got twelve months hard labour.

Nowhere is there a better example of the anachronism of the law than in the cases of fortune-telling that Abberline investigated. In Case 23, which has no date and no newspaper provenance, he is listed as being 'of the City Police but attached to the H Division'[!]. He also set up a sting which today would be construed as entrapment. He sent Mrs Eliza Sherington of Crispin Street and Miss Gertrude Riley of Nottingham Place for a consultation with forty-three year old Harriet Tannenbaum of Thomas Street, Commercial Road. The archaic charge in court read 'with intent to cheat and deceive divers of her Majesty's lieges.'

Mrs Tannenbaum, urging her clients to have nothing to do with courts and warrants (she'd been arrested twice before), told them both they would come into money and that Miss Riley would marry a man 'between colours'. They paid her 6d and she said she hoped it would be a sovereign next time. Some 652 playing cards were found on her premises, presumably Tarot packs, and some mystic German writing. Mrs Tannenbaum cut a rather pathetic figure in the dock, saying, 'Oh dear! Oh dear! My husband knew how to do it [tell fortunes] but not me.' Since *Mr* Tannenbaum was already doing time for the same offence, we have to wonder whether he had seen it coming! Harriet got six weeks hard labour.

'Obscene literature and Juvenile Depravity' screamed the newspaper headlines on one of Abberline's two pornography cases – a phrase that was bound to sell newspapers. Charles Newbold called himself Frederick Briggs when the need arose and he was selling indecent prints from his shop at 38 Wych Street off the Strand. Long before Soho acquired its reputation for vice, the west end of the Strand, Charing Cross and the arches of the Adelphi were known haunts of homosexuals, transvestites, prostitutes and purveyors of obscene literature. Abberline was working with Inspector Langrish and Chief Inspector John Shore on this one and, as with the fortune-tellers, he set Newbold up, this time posing as a punter himself and asking the price of various photographs in the shop. If Walter Dew was right about Abberline passing for a bank manager, Newbold was presumably off his guard.

Newspapers of the time were not allowed to be too explicit, so we have no idea of the exact content of the photos offered. In any case, categories of severity used by the Met's 'dirty squad' today have changed considerably since the 1880s. Even so, it was possible to buy photographs of naked women, men and children in various sexually explicit poses. Abberline must have been convincing because he asked Newbold to show him even stronger stuff, which emerged from behind a counter and for which of course the price went up. While Abberline was choosing – he eventually opted for five at four shillings each – Newbold flicked over the 'closed' sign. The transaction done, Abberline lifted the man off his feet and pushed him out of the shop door. When Newbold shouted 'Police!' he was promptly arrested by Sergeant Reader, who 'happened to be passing.'

The charge against Newbold was that he was 'maliciously selling and uttering to Frederick George Abberline, an inspector of the Metropolitan Police Force, in a public place, several obscene photographs and other articles against the statute ...' Newbold had little choice but to plead guilty and was given four months prison with hard labour.

Today, Frederick Abberline is best known for his work on the Ripper case of 1888–9. He was already at Scotland Yard by then but was recalled to Whitechapel because of his huge experience in the area. What he did not have, however, was much experience of murder. He only cites two in his cuttings and whereas one was successful, the other was not.

Henry Alt was hanged at Newgate by James Berry on 13 July 1885. As the executioner placed the white hood over his head and the noose around his neck, he shouted, 'This is all through an evil and deceitful woman.' Alt, a German journeyman baker, had stabbed Charles Howard to death over a quarrel over Mrs Eliza Russell, a widow whom they had both been courting. When Eliza turned Alt down in favour of Howard, he snapped and killed him, wounding both Eliza and himself in the process. The German Embassy, perhaps fearing an international incident, refused to get involved and Alt faced the gallows.

But no one faced the gallows for the murder of little Fanny Lazarus. In what the newspapers predictably termed 'The East End

Mystery', Elizabeth Lazarus, known as Fanny, went out to play with neighbours' children in New Castle Place, off Old Castle Street, on Wednesday, 29 May 1878. She was nineteen months old but, according to Abberline, 'very forward and tall' and her killer may have taken her to be much older than she was. When the child had not returned home by six o'clock, her father, a tailor who lived at 4 New Castle Place, reported her missing to the police. The little girl's description was circulated in the area but there were no sightings until 1.15am on the morning of Saturday 1 June when three men, converging separately on New Castle Place, found her body lying on the doorstep of No. 22, only a few doors away from her house. They called a patrolling constable whose name and number are not given in the newspaper reports and he noted that the body was wet from head to waist but the lower trunk, legs and feet were dry. The little girl was still clothed. The inquest on Fanny Lazarus was held at the Weavers' Arms, Baker's Row on Monday, 9 June. It remained a bone of contention with coroners and police officers alike that there were not enough specialist buildings in London and coroners had to hold court wherever they could. Joseph Barnett, a cigar-maker of 9 Old Castle Street, gave evidence to coroner Hannay about his finding the body and Dr Edward Crouch, H Division's assistant police surgeon, described its condition. Her body was covered in fine sand. Her hair was matted with it and there was some in her mouth and nostrils. Her tongue was pro-truding and he believed the cause of death was suffocation by drowning. The inquest was adjourned to allow Inspector Abberline more time to investigate.

He went to the crime scene with Sergeant Foster and noted that building works were going on in Goulston Square and Castle Alley (where Alice McKenzie's body would be found eleven years later). Here stood two wooden tubs containing sand and water. Abberline was sure he had the actual murder site and that the murderer would not be far away. He arrested sixty-two-year-old night watchman Peter Wincey 'for causing the death of a child' but since evidence against the man was flimsy, he was remanded on his own bail.

At two o'clock on the Saturday that Fanny Lazarus had been found, Peter Wincey called at her house and asked Simon Lazarus if he could see the body. The request perhaps was not as strange then as it would be today. Corpses routinely were laid out in parlours and friends and neighbours came to pay their respects. Simon Lazarus did not know the man and his behaviour in the next few minutes was decidedly odd. He felt the little girl's legs and head and began to tremble before collapsing into a chair with his head in his hands. 'Leave it all to me,' he said to the bewildered father, 'and I will make it all right.' He asked Simon to show him where the body had been found and when they got there, Wincey said, 'No, it was the middle step.' He then left but came back later and said to Simon Lazarus, 'You must give me your name and address and you must come when I send for you.'

Wincey lived in Goulston Street and was a night watchman and time-keeper at the public baths and wash houses in Castle Alley (the front wall still stands). His shift ran from 5.30pm when the builders 'knocked off' until 7.00am the next morning. When the inquest was resumed, Wincey was cautioned by the coroner and said that he had been on duty in the early hours of 1 June and had heard a disturbance outside. He had gone out to investigate, but could see nothing and had returned to the baths. This was just as well because Joseph Barnett said he saw someone resembling Wincey walking towards the wash-house, i.e. away from the body.

Coroner Hannay wanted to know why Wincey had gone to the Lazarus house. Simon Lazarus had let him in because he assumed he was a parish officer merely carrying out his duties. Wincey, an 'educated, professional man' despite his humble status, said he was a father of nine and had gone there out of sympathy. He denied having promised to 'make everything all right.'

A local man, Moses Isaacs, testified that he had often seen Wincey chasing off annoying children with a stick. At the end of the day, Hannay came out with a conclusion which must be uniquely bizarre in the annals of coroners' proceedings. He saw no reason to believe that the child had drowned accidentally and had been fished out by someone and 'been secreted' until being found. The matter, he said, could be reopened if the police found more evidence. Surprisingly, given the clear – if preposterous – nudge by the coroner, the jury returned a verdict of 'wilful murder by person or persons unknown'. They obviously believed Mr Hannay was a few pieces of evidence short of a verdict.

Abberline and Foster must have been fuming. Had the girl fallen into the tub accidentally, she would have been wet from head to foot, not merely from the waist up. Had someone – perhaps an older playmate – fished her out before she got wet below the waist, she would not have gulped enough water to kill her. The physical evidence was clear – someone had upended little Fanny Lazarus in the water-butt until she drowned. They had then taken the body and hidden it somewhere (probably cold) until they found the opportunity to dump it. There seems to have been no discussion of the time of death, so the girl could have died at any time between Wednesday night and early Saturday morning. The fact that Wincey was seen yards from the body at the appropriate time and was known to be short-tempered with children may be merely circumstantial, but his bizarre and creepy behaviour with Fanny's corpse points to something more sinister than a man who loses his composure with the bad behaviour of local kids. He fondled the girl's legs and head and knew *exactly* on which step the body was found.

Not for the first or last time, Inspector Frederick Abberline was obliged to let a guilty man go free.

Shortly before Christmas 1887, Abberline finally gave in to pressure from 'Dolly' Williamson and James Monro and joined A Division as a prelude to joining the Commissioner's Office at Scotland Yard. The building itself was bursting at the seams and everybody no doubt longed to be able to stretch their legs by moving into Norman Shaw's Opera House, currently being built along the Embankment.[11]

Abberline's leaving H Division after fourteen years was a wrench, but as he himself said it gave him opportunity for promotion and pastures new. A dinner was held in his honour at the Unicorn Tavern along Shoreditch High Street. The barrister George Hay Young was in the chair and in his speech told everyone that he had known Abberline for years and hated to see him in court because he knew, as defence counsel, he was in for an uphill battle! The inspector was, he said: 'most careful, painstaking and upright in all his work – neither leaning to the right nor to the left ... the ideal of a faithful, conscientious officer.'[12]

Abberline was given a gold, keyless hunter watch and a large amount of cash. On the watch was inscribed 'Presented together with a purse of gold to Inspector F.G. Abberline by the inhabitants of Spitalfields, Whitechapel etc on his leaving the district after fourteen years.'

Among the many toasts delivered that evening was one by R.A. Kearsey, who raised his glass to:

The Metropolitan Police. I pay the highest eulogium to the police of H Division – from the Superintendent down to the humblest constable – for their ready assistance at all times and their civility and attention to the desires of the inhabitants.

As for Abberline, Superintendent Arnold said, 'A better officer there could not be.' No one could know that within eight months, Abberline would be back and he would need all the friends he could get.

Chapter 6

Hunting Jack

The Whitechapel murderer had struck twice – or was it three times? – before they sent for Abberline. One of the many problems confronting the researcher on Jack the Ripper – to use the infamous 'trade name' on a letter sent to the Central News Agency in late September 1888 – is exactly how many women did Jack kill?

We can discount 'Fairy Fay', reputedly murdered on Boxing Day 1887. She was almost certainly a creation of the rabid, sensation-hungry 'new journalism', anxious to win the readership war at all costs. Annie Millwood was attacked on the afternoon of Saturday, 25 February in broad daylight by a man with a clasp knife. Though admitted to the Whitechapel Workhouse Infirmary she recovered, only to die the following month from natural, unrelated causes. The motive for the attack and the assailant remain unknown, but he is unlikely to have been the Ripper. Ada Wilson was attacked in her own home in Maidman Street, Mile End, by a knife-wielding man who tried to rob her. She recovered. Emma Smith was not so lucky. On Bank Holiday Monday, 2 April, she was accosted by three men outside the Chocolate and Mustard Mill on the intersection of Wentworth Street and Brick Lane. She was badly beaten, her ear almost torn off and a sharp object, perhaps a stick, forced into her vagina. The youngest of her attackers, she told police, was about nineteen. She died from peritonitis two days later.

Martha Tabram, aka Turner, was different. Certainly the Press of the day and many senior policemen, including Abberline, assumed that she was the Ripper's first victim. There is some doubt about Annie Millwood, Ada Wilson and Emma Smith, but Martha Tabram was definitely a prostitute. She had gone with a soldier, possibly Private Skipper of the Coldstream Guards, up George Yard, the gloomy, narrow passageway known as Shit Alley, in the early hours of Tuesday, 7 August. Her body was found on a landing at George Yard Buildings at 4.50am and she had been subjected to no fewer than thirty-nine knife wounds. Her throat had been cut – the trademark of the man who would come to be known as Jack the Ripper.

The real hysteria started with the murder of Mary Ann Nichols, known as Polly, on the night of Friday, 31 August. She was found by carman Charles Cross lying on the pavement outside the locked gates of Brown's Stable Yard in Buck's Row (today, Durward Street). Her throat had been cut but the extent of her abdominal mutilations would not become evident until she was stripped at the Whitechapel Infirmary Mortuary in Eagle Place some three minutes walk away. Dr Rees Llewellyn had been called to the crime scene and now Inspector John Spratling of J Division called him to the mortuary. 'A keen eyed man with iron grey hair and beard', as *The Star* newspaper was to describe him in September, was horrified by Polly's wounds, as was Llewellyn, who told the Press, 'I have seen many terrible cases but never such a brutal affair as this.' There were two vicious cuts across the throat and the carotid arteries on both sides had been severed. The killer had probably used what we call today a blitz attack, a fast grip of the throat leading to partial unconsciousness, followed by cuts to the throat while she was on the ground. The abdominal cuts were deep and jagged and Llewellyn was the first to express his belief that the murderer had some rough anatomical knowledge, for he seemed to have attacked all the vital parts.

Since Polly Nichols died on J Division's patch, Inspector Spratling and his fellow officers got straight to work to find out who the dead woman was and to try to piece together the last days and hours of her life. Their work at the time has been augmented by serious research over the last thirty years and, today, Jack's victims are as well-chronicled as any titled lady in the land. Polly was forty-five years old and five feet two inches tall, with five teeth missing, giving her in life a slightly gormless expression. She was the daughter of a locksmith, had been married and had given birth to five children between 1866 and 1879. The marriage – to painter William Nichols – was not a happy one and she started drinking. By 1880 the pair had separated and Polly took to the streets to earn a living. She was in and out of workhouses and doss-houses for the last eight years of her life and was sleeping rough in Trafalgar Square the previous November when Sir Charles Warren had sent in the Met backed by the army to clear the place of the down and outs who were threatening to take it over. Her last chance to crawl out of the gutter came in the summer of 1888 when she went to work as a servant for a respectable family in Wandsworth. But she stole clothes from them worth £3 10s and ran.

For most of August, Polly slept in a doss house at 18 Thrawl Street, where her hard wooden bed cost her 4d a night. In the week before her death she was dossing at the White House, 56 Flower and Dean Street. J Division detectives interviewed scores of people and drew up a timeframe which became a countdown to murder. At 12.30am on the morning of Friday, 31 August, a drunk Polly wandered away from the Frying Pan pub on the corner of Thrawl Street and Brick Lane. At 1.20am the deputy of the Thrawl Street doss house refused to admit her because she had no money for her bed. 'I'll soon get my doss money,' she told him. 'See what a jolly bonnet I've got now.'

At shortly after 3.30am, while residents of the East End watched the glow in the sky from the fire at Gibbs and Co. in Shadwell Dry Dock, fellow prostitute Ellen Holland saw Polly at the corner of Brick Lane and Osborne Street, by coincidence the scene of the three-man attack on Emma Smith months earlier. Polly had no intention of going back to Thrawl Street. She was going to 'Flowery Dean' because the wards there were mixed. Instead, she met Jack.

Something akin to panic set in a week later when a second 'unfortunate' was found slaughtered and this time the mutilations were truly appalling. Forty-six-year-old Annie Chapman lay at the bottom of the three steps that led down into a yard at the back of 29 Hanbury Street, perhaps five or six minutes walk from the murder site of Polly Nichols. The timing of the find meant that her killer had struck at around 5.00am, when the day was well and truly breaking. Although the residents of No. 29 denied it later, the passage that led from the front door to the yard at the back was frequently used by prostitutes and their clients because the door was never locked and the yard was secluded.

By 6.10am, Inspector Joseph Chandler of H Division knew of the murder and got himself to Hanbury Street in a hurry. He found Annie

> lying on her back, dead, left arm resting on left breast, legs drawn up, abducted, small intestines and flap of the abdomen lying on right side, above right shoulder, attached to a cord with the rest of the intestines inside the body; two flaps of skin from the lower part of the abdomen lying in a large quantity of blood above the right shoulder; throat cut deeply from left and back in a jagged manner right around throat.[1]

Once the body had been taken by hand-drawn ambulance to the Whitechapel Workhouse Infirmary mortuary, Chandler made a careful inspection of the murder scene. There were blood spatters and patches of varying sizes on the wall of the house and the wooden fence that separated No. 29 from next door. Near where Annie's corpse had lain he found an envelope containing two tablets and carrying the crest of the Sussex Regiment. Part of a name and address were still visible on it and it was postmarked 'London, Aug 23 1888'. There were two combs and a piece of muslin cloth lying there, as though they had spilled from the dead woman's pockets. While he compiled his report, blissfully unaware as everyone was of fingerprinting, DNA evidence and all the modern forensics that would almost certainly have caught Jack today, Dr Bagster Phillips went to work in the makeshift mortuary. The medical journal *The Lancet* was the only publication allowed to print the following details from Phillips's report:

> The abdomen had been entirely laid open, the intestines, severed from their mesenteric attachments, had been lifted out of the body and placed by the shoulder of the corpse ... the posterior two thirds of the bladder had been entirely removed.

As with Llewellyn's opinion on the killer of Polly Nichols, Phillips concluded that Annie's murderer 'had such knowledge of anatomical or pathological examinations as to be enabled to secure the pelvic organs with one sweep of the knife.'

Although the concept of the trophy-hunting serial killer was not understood at the time, Jack was turning out to be the sexually-impelled sadistic murderer that is a classic of its type. And some-body that hysterical Saturday decided to send for Inspector Abberline.

The reasons for this are obvious enough, but it was rather ironic bearing in mind that Williamson and Monro had been trying for years to get the man to *leave* Whitechapel; they were now sending him back. There was no one else with Abberline's experience of the area, so naturally he headed up the team, but he was not the only detective sent from the Yard; nor was he ever 'in charge' of the case. We will look at the chain of command later, but Abberline was unquestionably the senior man in charge of the detectives on the ground and knew the rabbit-warren of the Abyss like the back of his hand.

Into the Abyss with him went fellow inspector Henry Moore, who had been a railway employee and a silk warehouseman prior to joining the Met in 1869. He was five years younger than Abberline, but his rise was just as rapid. From patrolling the beat in W Division (Clapham) he was promoted to sergeant in 1878 and transferred to P Division (Peckham). Three years later he transferred to the CID and had only just arrived at Scotland Yard in the months before the Ripper struck. He had no working knowledge of Whitechapel and little affinity with the people of the Abyss. On his retirement in 1899 he let his hair down on the subject in the *Police Review*:

> The class of woman we had to deal with have told any number of stories for a shilling and it was impossible to believe any woman, owing to the hysterical state of fear they get themselves into ... We have in the East End foreigners from every corner of the earth and when they hate, they will tell such lies as would make your hair stand on end.

The other officer sent with Abberline to Whitechapel was Inspector Walter Andrews, a Suffolk man who had joined the Met in 1869. He was four years younger than Abberline and Walter Dew, a young constable at the time of the Ripper case, remembered him as 'a jovial, gentlemanly man, with a fine personality and a sound knowledge of his job.'[2]

Oddly there is no mention of Andrews working the case in the Scotland Yard files (there are huge gaps in these through pilfering by researchers) and we know that Andrews was in Toronto in December 1888 escorting fraudster Roland Barrett back for trial from London where he had been arrested.[3] At this point, Andrews told a journalist, there were twenty-three detectives, two clerks and one inspector working the Whitechapel murder case. This may be true of *December* (by which time Jack's killing spree seemed to have abated), but it is not likely to be accurate for the previous three months. Even if Dew was wrong about Andrews, there were two inspectors from the Yard (Abberline and Moore) apart from the local men in H and J divisions. Who else was in Abberline's team? On 12 November, *The Times* reported that inspectors Reid and Nearn, along with sergeants Thick, McCarthy, Godley and Pearce had been working closely under him for weeks. Edward Reid was the shortest man in the Met at five feet six inches and one of the most colourful. He had taken over from Abberline as local inspector the year before the Ripper killings and he was something of a renaissance man. He had been a ship's steward and pastry cook (along with fifteen other 'careers') prior to joining the Met, which he did in 1872. Like many of the brightest, his promotion was rapid. He joined the CID of P Division in 1874, was a sergeant four years later and an inspector at the Yard by 1884. When the new J Division was set up in Bethnal Green two years later, Reid was sent to organize it.

What was unusual about Reid was his extracurricular activities. He was a first-class conjuror, had a beautiful tenor singing voice and was no mean actor. He was also addicted to the trend of ballooning, which swept the country in the 1870s and 1880s, and made twenty-three ascents from the Alexandra and Crystal palaces throughout his career. He received a gold medal for a record ascent five years before the Ripper case and bailed out of a balloon in a parachute 1,000 feet above the ground at a fair in Luton. What was unique about Reid was that he was the hero of a series of novels written by his friend, the Scottish author Charles Gibbon. Whereas Arthur Conan Doyle would create a series of fictional CID men, with Lestrade as 'the best of a bad bunch', Detective Sergeant Dier was simply Reid spelled backwards. The novels were said to be among the favourites of the queen and, although they are obscure today, it is quite extraordinary that nobody seems to have commented on the connection at the time. Presumably, Gibbon's stories are simply flights of fancy and not actually based on snippets of real cases that Reid might have been slipping him. A photograph taken in the 1880s shows Reid as a plump man with kindly eyes and a waxed moustache. Like Abberline, he dressed well but had the demeanour of a bank manager.

James Nearn was nothing like so high profile. He had joined the Met in September 1877 and was presented with a pipe inscribed 'Souvenir to James Nearn, Whitechapel Murders, 1888, from six brother officers' (one of whom may have been Abberline). He scarcely merits a mention in books on the Ripper case, even those which focus specifically on police activities, and it may be that he was a back-room boy coordinating paperwork rather than walking the streets in pursuit of Jack.

Sergeant William Thick is far better known. He was two years younger than Abberline and joined the Met in 1868. He served in B and P Divisions (Chelsea and Peckham) before returning to H Division where he had started. He is described as stout, but the photograph of him in the 1880s shows a well-built man with a firm jaw and luxurious blond moustaches. Sergeant John McCarthy served with G Division (King's Cross) before obtaining a clerkship at Scotland Yard. Three years before the Ripper case he was posted to the Convict Supervision Office, where he would have checked on ticket-of-leave men newly released. Abberline's cases over the years make constant references to this police supervision programme, with a number of years added to the felons' prison sentences.

Sergeant George Godley has, like Abberline himself, achieved a kind of immortality in film, firstly through Lewis Collins in Michael Caine's *Jack the Ripper* and secondly through Robbie Coltrane in Johnny Depp's *From Hell*. Other than in film fiction, there is nothing to suppose that Abberline and Godley were a 'pair' in the accepted sense. Originally from Sussex, Godley had served with J Division and the only official surviving report of him in the Ripper case to that date was that he had investigated the statement of Mary Ann Connelly, 'Pearly Poll', who was a friend of Martha Tabram murdered in George Yard. Typical of the casual reporting of the time, the *Echo* of 20 September 1888 spells his name Goadby.

Sergeant Albert Pearce is a name only. He joined the Met in 1881 and was part of Abberline's team. That is all we can say about him on 8 September 1888, although in the following July he would take statements from eye-witnesses Margaret Franklin and Elizabeth Ryder when investigating the murder of 'Clay Pipe' Alice McKenzie.

So what happened from that September day on? Since Abberline is today the most famous policeman involved in the hunt for Jack the Ripper, we need to know exactly what he did. And that, of course, poses problems. If his name is not there – if Reid or Thick or Godley interviewed suspects and witnesses for example – we get the impression that he is doing nothing. What we have to remember is that Frederick Abberline was an extraordinarily dedicated officer. We know from his *Reminiscences* that he often worked long into the night, at Commercial Street or Leman Street stations, before writing up various reports longhand. We also know that he personally wandered the Abyss, talking to the street women and giving them the 4d they needed for a bed, just to get them off those streets and safely away from Jack's knife. Whatever his team were doing in the weeks of the Whitechapel murders, Abberline was reading every statement, directing affairs, following up clues and becoming more and more frustrated at the brick walls he found himself facing.

On the day that Annie Chapman was found, a number of officers were put into plain clothes. The general feeling of most writers on the Ripper case today is that the public were enormously helpful to the police in their enquiries. That does not square with Inspector Moore's memories above and neither is it likely. Of course there were respectable people in the Abyss, but many of them were new-comers from Eastern Europe, men and women who had run from the police states of Russia and Poland and would have had no love for a man in uniform. Perhaps this was why Inspector Chandler, Sergeant Lee and constables Barrett, Cooke, Hussey, Schnelzer, Sziemanowicz and White, all of H Division, found themselves con-ducting enquiries in 'civvies'. If this was Abberline's decision, he must have hit the ground running, coordinating the follow-up to the Chapman murder with a frenetic efficiency. All seventeen of the inhabitants of 29 Hanbury Street were interviewed. Pawnbrokers were checked to find any trace of the rings apparently torn from the dead woman's finger. The envelope with the Sussex regimental crest was followed up by Chandler, who was sent by Abberline to the regimental headquarters at Farnborough, Sussex.

Prostitutes were interviewed; men known to be anywhere in the immediate area at the time; the finders of the body. Above all, it was clear to Abberline that the killer of Annie Chapman was also the killer of Polly Nichols and of Martha Tabram and he began to co-ordinate all three in an attempt to find a pattern. In fact, a report on Polly Nichols compiled by Inspector John Helson of J Division reads:

> The enquiry is being carefully continued, by Inspector Abberline from C.O. [Commissioner's Office, i.e. Scotland Yard] and myself and every effort made to obtain information that may lead to arrest of the murderer.[4]

These were the days of optimism before the whole investigation stalled, but the report is dated 7 September, the day before Abberline took up his duties. *Exactly* when he began to investigate is unknown.

He also constantly had to feed back to his superiors at Scotland Yard, where Chief Inspector Donald Swanson was trying to make sense of it all. Swanson does not feature in any of the films about Jack the Ripper and that is a shame because he was a clever and efficient police officer. Born and educated in Scotland, Swanson was a clerk in the City before joining the Met in 1868. He was half an inch taller than Abberline and five years younger, serving in no fewer than four Divisions before joining Commissioner's Office nearly a year before Jack struck. In 1881 he achieved fame by arresting Percy Lefroy, the railway murderer. He was modest and unassuming, strongly disapproving of 'celebrities' like Reid, and he played his cards close to his chest. Much of the reporting of the Ripper case bears his signature, but most of it came via Abberline as his eyes and ears on the ground.

One particular suspect that Abberline followed up was the man behaving madly in the Prince Albert pub on the corner of Bushfield Street and Steward Street some hour and a half after Annie Chapman was murdered. Mrs Fiddymont, the landlady, remembered that his shirt was torn and he had blood on his right hand and ear. Mary Chappell was there too and Mrs Fiddymont asked her to stay with her, unnerved by the man's wild appearance – 'startling and terrifying'. Another drinker at the Prince Albert, builder Joseph Tailor, followed the odd man as far as Half Moon Street, Bishopsgate, alarmed by his erratic manner and strange, springy step.

Three days after Annie Chapman died, two doctors from Holloway, Cowan and Crabb, told police that they believed the killer was Jacob Isenschmid, a pork butcher who lived nearby. The police in Holloway held him on 12 September and by the 18th he was being detained at Bow Infirmary Asylum in Fairfield Road, Bow. Abberline's report on the man has survived and it is clear that Isenschmid was the same man seen by Mrs Fiddymont and others in the Prince Albert. Abberline was clearly anxious to have him identified formally by the landlady, but his doctors were not happy about this. Even 'Dolly' Williamson had been to see the doctor, but the net result was delay. Abberline had found out that Isenschmid had a history of bouts of violence. As a butcher he habitually carried knives and, despite having a wife and home, had been lodging with a Mr Tyler of 60 Milford Road since 5 September. His whereabouts on the night of the Chapman murder were unknown.

The spadework had been done by Sergeant Thick. He talked to Mrs Isenschmid on 12 September and was able to write a potted history of the man. He had been married for twenty-one years and ran a pork butcher's shop at 59 Elthorne Road, Upper Holloway. When the business failed, Isenschmid became depressed and started wandering the streets. He had spent several weeks in Colney Hatch Lunatic Asylum and when released, supposedly cured, worked for a butcher in Marylebone High Street. This did not last and Isenschmid's visits home became less and less frequent. He was occasionally picked up by the police for vagrancy. Mrs Isenschmid did not think her husband would hurt anyone but her – 'I think he would kill me if he had the chance'. Generally known as the 'mad butcher', Isenschmid drank in a German-run pub in Wentworth Street, Whitechapel, although his precise reason for loitering in that particular area was not established. Like every other policeman at the time, Abberline had no idea what made serial killers tick. Even the term was unknown; men who killed more than once were called habitual homicides. Some of them, we now know, kill other women in lieu of their wives[5] and all the victims so far had been

Mrs Isenschmid's approximate age. It is not clear whether Mrs Fiddymont ever did get to see the mad pork butcher, but since he was in Colney Hatch during the later spate of Whitechapel murders, Abberline would have had no choice but to rule him out.

Abberline was too good a copper to sit on his hands assuming the crime was solved and he focussed on the medical aspects of the murders. The three insane medical students sound like a rather bizarre music hall act, but no policeman in London in 1888 could afford to leave any stone unturned. It is not clear how these men came to the notice of Abberline's team, or indeed who two of them were. The third, however, was John Sanders of 20 Abercorn Road, Maida Vale and, like the others, he was a student at the London Hospital, virtually across the road from the murder site of Polly Nichols. Abberline sent a detective (possibly Sergeant Frank Froest) to his last known address at Aberdeen Place, St John's Wood. He was too late – the Sanderses had gone.

Diligent research over the years, however, has shown that Sanders had joined the staff at the hospital in 1879 working as an outpatient dresser (or casualty officer as we would call him today). A few months before the Whitechapel killings started, Sanders became prone to fits of violence, attacking his friends. It stood to reason that, as a fledgling doctor, he had access to scalpels and Abberline wanted to be sure. In fact, Sanders was already in an asylum at West Malling Place in Kent and could not possibly have been Jack.

There were probably no more peculiar characters wandering the streets of the Abyss in 1888 than at any other time, but because of the murders, the spotlight of both the police and the Press is thrown on them and they stand out in sharp relief. Certainly the alienation of a great, impersonal city did not help and, although London is said to be actually a series of little villages, Whitechapel was too global for this. There were, after all, nearly half a million people there and the fact that various witnesses in the Ripper case were describing men they did not know is a reminder of the sheer scale of Abberline's problem. Even by 19 September, before Jack continued his work, the pressure on the police to arrest a suspect was huge. Abberline said so himself in a report written that day: 'time is of the greatest importance in this case, not only with regard to the question of

81

identity, but also for the purpose of allaying the strong public feeling that exists.'[6]

And by that time, Abberline had already felt the collar of William Henry Piggott. At 4.00pm on the afternoon of Sunday, 9 September, the day after Annie Chapman died, Piggott, variously described as a publican and a ship's cook, turned up at the Pope's Head pub in Gravesend, behaving oddly and loudly shouting about his hatred of women. The police were called and Superintendent Berry asked the man about his recent hand injury. Piggott told him it had been bitten by a woman in Brick Lane, Whitechapel. She had collapsed in a fit at half past four that morning and in trying to help her, she had misunderstood the situation and attacked him. He hit her and ran. A bag he had unaccountably left in a Gravesend fish shop contained a shirt with blood spots on it. The local police surgeon believed that blood had recently been wiped from Piggott's boots.

When Abberline arrived on Monday morning he arrested Pigott on suspicion and took him back to Whitechapel by train to London Bridge and then four-wheeler to Commercial Street, to take part in an identity parade in front of Mrs Fiddymont, Mary Chappell and Joseph Tailor, who had witnessed the odd behaviour of the man in the Prince Albert on the previous day. Mary Chappell was the only witness who was unsure; the others completely failed to recognize him. Pigott was taken to the Whitechapel Workhouse Infirmary where Dr Larter, the resident physician, treated him for delirium tremens. He was released on 9 October.

Like Isenschmid, Pigott proved to be another red herring. By that Monday, seven men were helping the police with their enquiries and the frustration in all ranks was beginning to show. Three days later, a Friedrich Schumacher was arrested and taken to Leman Street. In what might have been a punch-up at the station, a woman's bundle of clothes was destroyed and the owner herself got some rough handling. Inspector Charles Pinhorn of H Division got his knuckles rapped[7] and Sergeant New was demoted and transferred.

On 14 October, Abberline was looking very closely at Edward McKenna. His report to Swanson makes it clear that the pedlar resembled a man seen openly carrying a knife in Heath Street and Flower and Dean Street. Abberline questioned him at Commercial

Street Station. McKenna was Abberline's height with sandy hair and beard and wore a skull cap (though it was unlikely he was Jewish). His worldly belongings were listed as: rags, two women's purses, several metal and cardboard boxes, handkerchiefs, a leather strap and a spring onion. In fact, McKenna had an alibi. He was asleep at a doss house at 15 Brick Lane on the night of the Chapman killing and Abberline had no option but to let him go.

During these frantic days following the death of Annie Chapman, Abberline's team also picked up John Fitzgerald, who confessed to the killing on the 26th. He was a plasterer by trade and probably one of those serial confessors who loves the limelight. He was released three days later. 'Mary' was a different kind of criminal, a male hairdresser with a record of sex offences against girls and young women. Exactly who he was and why he should have been considered a suspect is unknown, but his case involved Abberline's people contacting the German police in Bremen, only to be told that 'Mary' was serving a twelve-month stretch in Oslebshausen gaol. It is possible that he was Theophil Mary, born in Alsace in 1851.

Pressure was coming from above as well as without. The chain of command above Swanson began with the Home Secretary, Henry Matthews. The first Catholic since the Reformation to reach Cabinet rank, Matthews was an able lawyer but unpopular and probably out of his depth at the tip of politics. His boss, Lord Salisbury, the Prime Minister, wrote to the queen 'there is an innocence of the ways of the world which no one could have expected to find in a civil lawyer of sixty'[8] and he probably regretted appointing him. Below him came Sir Charles Warren, Commissioner at the Yard. Warren was an Engineer officer in the army and amateur archaeologist. Since it was still the norm for military men to become commissioners of police, the appointment in 1886 was generally welcomed. By 1888, however, he had blotted his copybook, badly handing the riots in Trafalgar Square in November 1887 when yet another 'Bloody Sunday' saw the people in a pitched battle with the Met and the Guards. More importantly, he clashed with almost everybody he had to work with, from Matthews to James Monro, Head of the CID, to Godfrey Lushington, the Home Officer Liaison Secretary to his own successor, the incredibly amiable Colonel Edward Bradford. When he whinged a week after his resignation in November that the public acted in their complaints against the Met as if the police were doing nothing, he was defending men like Abberline. But it was his own almost paranoid secrecy (echoed, admittedly, by Monro) that led to a complete clampdown on information from the police. As far as the bulk of the public knew, they *were* doing nothing.

Warren's unbelievable arrogance is shown by his letter to Acting Assistant Commissioner, Alexander Carmichael Bruce, in which he wrote: 'I go so far as to say that I could myself in a few days unravel the mystery [the Whitechapel murders] provided I could spare the time and give individual attention to it.'[9]

It is probably as well that Abberline and his team never got to see this letter.

In the midst of all this back-biting and unhelpful recriminations, Henry Matthews urged his secretary, Evelyn Ruggles-Brise, to 'stimulate the Police about Whitechapel murders.'[10] It seems an odd memo to send if information was being sent up the line the other way, i.e. from detectives in the field to the Yard to Whitehall, but it was not helped by the physical absence of Robert Anderson, Assistant Commissioner at the Yard, who had been sent to Switzerland for the good of his health (!) on the day that Abberline took on the Chapman case.

In practice, the men who operated above Swanson were Dolly Williamson, overworked, unwell and a more bitter man than he used to be, and Superintendent John Shore. Shore's name appears on various documents in the Ripper Files[11], but he appears to have had little actual involvement. There is a sense that Shore had been promoted above his abilities. The anti-establishment newspaper, William Stead's *Pall Mall Gazette*, described him as a 'rough diamond from Gloucestershire', implying that he was absolutely the wrong man to be hunting Jack.

Then, on the night of 30 September, two women, fifteen minutes walk apart, were murdered by the same hand. Jack was back.

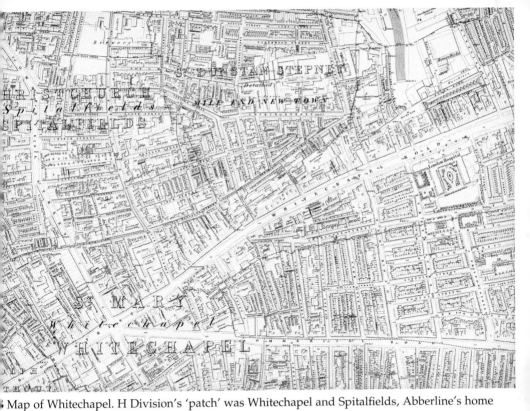

Map of Whitechapel. H Division's 'patch' was Whitechapel and Spitalfields, Abberline's home fourteen years.

Punch magazine – (*Left*) 'The Burglarian Question'. Sir Charles Warren, Commissioner of Police, comes under fire for failing to cope with crime, 1886. (*Right*) 'Bull's Eye on Bobby', August 1877. The Trial of the Detectives in 1887 exposed corruption in the Metropolitan Police.

THE BURGLARIAN QUESTION.

Mr. Punch. "BRAVO, SIR CHARLES! YOU'VE DONE CAPITALLY WITH THE DOGS AND DEMOCRATS. HOW ABOUT THE *BURGLARS*?"
Chief Commissioner of Police. "ALL RIGHT, MR. PUNCH! 'MUCH HAS BEEN DONE, BUT MORE REMAINS TO"!"

BULL'S EYE ON BOBBY.

Mr. Bull (*takes Policeman's lantern*). "THANK YOU. I'LL JUST HAVE A LOOK ROUND MYSELF. STRIKES ME THE PREMISES AIN'T AS CLEAN AS THEY MIGHT BE!"

Why I did not write my Reminiscences when I retired from the Metropolitan Police.

I think it is just as well to record here the Reason why as from the various cuttings from the Newspapers as well as the many other matters that I was called upon to investigate – that never became public property – it must be apparent that I could write many things that would be very interesting to read.

At the time I retired from the Service the Authorities were very much opposed to retired Officers writing anything for the press as previously some retired Officers had from time to time been very indiscreet in what they had caused to be published and to my knowledge had been called upon

A page from Abberline's Press Cuttings. The handwriting is totally different from that of the supposed 'Diaries' of G.F. Abberline.

ederick George Abberline's birth certificate, January 1843.

SCENE IN BOW St POLICE COURT

he Trial of the Dynamitards, 1885. The suspects Cunningham and Burton are in profile on the left.

HARRY. BURTON

CUNNINGHAM

The Dynamitards, Burton and Cunningham, at their trial in 1885. Abberline says that the likenesses are very good.

The best-known artist's impression of Abberline at the time of the dynamite case. Note the spelling of the name.

Superintendent Thomas Arnold was head of Whitechapel's H Division and effectively Abberline's boss.

ABERLINE

ARNOLD

The baby farmers Joseph and Annie Roodhouse in the dock.

The docker's wife who adopted a baby 'all for love' as typical of the babyfarmers' victims.

'Photograph' of the con-man Walter Selwyn (aka Retlaw Newles). He was probably the last man to be arrested by Frederick Abberline and this image comes from his cuttings.

The site of the Unicorn Tavern, where a dinner was held in Abberline's honour on his leaving H Division in 1887. (© *Eloise Campbell*)

The Whitechapel Baths and Wash-house looked down on the murder site of Fanny Lazarus. The attendant here, Robert Wincey, was almost certainly her killer. (© *Eloise Campbell*)

...berline was born in Salisbury Street, Blandford Forum, a town almost destroyed by fire. (© *Carol Trow*)

...lock made by Robert Hood of ...ndford, to whom Abberline may ...e been apprenticed before joining ... police. (© *Carol Trow*)

Hannah Abberline's shop in East Street, Blandford. The window is largely unchanged from the 1850s. (© *Carol Trow*)

New Scotland Yard, Abberline's HQ for the last year of his career. (© *Eloise Campbell*)

The grave of Frederick and Emma Abberline with the new headstone, erected in 2007. (© *Carol Trow*)

In Memory of
Frederick George Abberline
8 January 1843 (Blandford Forum)
- 10 December 1929 (Bournemouth)
Chief Inspector CID Scotland Yard
And his wife
Emma Abberline née Beament
26 September 1844 (Islington)
- 15 March 1930 (Bournemouth)

Chapter 7

Lost in Theories

The 'double event' of 30 September not only cranked up the hysteria in the East End, but it also brought the City of London force directly into the case and added enormously to the ongoing legend of Jack the Ripper.

Six days earlier, a letter had been sent to Sir Charles Warren claiming to be from the Whitechapel murderer. It was unsigned and the envelope had a London SE postmark. It was the first of some 220 letters and postcards addressed to the police or the Press which purported to be the killer's handiwork; but it was the second letter which began the legend. 'Dear Boss,' it began and gave the most obvious motive for the murders – 'I am down on whores.' It was an arrogant, boastful letter, probably penned by a journalist named Bulling or Best (the jury is still out on the precise authorship) and it gave the now infamous 'trade name', 'Yours truly, Jack the Ripper'. From now on, Abberline would not just be hunting the Whitechapel murderer; he would be hunting a phenomenon.

Elizabeth Stride was found dead by travelling salesman Louis Diemschutz as he turned his pony and trap into the narrow entranceway of Dutfield's Yard along Berner Street. It was about 1.00am and Diemschutz's pony shied at what looked like a pile of rags to the right of the gate. Diemschutz got down, struck a match and saw a woman staring up at him through sightless eyes, her throat cut and her blood still trickling into the gutter. He dashed up the stairs to the International Working Men's Club on the first floor. He was a regular here and his friend Isaac Kozebrodsky went back down to the yard with him. Then they ran for a patrolling policeman.

The first medical man on the scene was Edward Johnston, assistant to Dr Frederick Blackwell of 100 Commercial Road.

Johnston noted that the woman's body was still warm and that her bonnet lay near her head. At 1.16am by his own watch, Dr Blackwell arrived and, in keeping with the newly-established principles of Dr Virchow of Berlin, made a careful examination of the crime scene and the corpse. Liz Stride lay on her left, facing the right wall of the alleyway with her feet nine feet from the gates themselves. Her right hand lay on her chest and was bloody. Her left was clenched around a packet of cachous (perfumed sweets). Her mouth was slightly open and the scarf around her neck had been pulled tight, perhaps as a ligature. Her throat had been cut with a single sweep cutting the windpipe in two. There were no further wounds or mutilations.

Dr Bagster Phillips, the police surgeon to H Division, arrived next, estimating the time of death from the approximate body temperature at between 12.44 and 12.54pm. Most experts today tend to the belief that Liz's killer was crouching behind the open gates of the yard when Diemschutz arrived and made good his escape, heading west in panic, while the salesman was upstairs summoning help. This was what the police suspected, but theorists over the years have reasoned that Liz Stride was not a Ripper victim, merely the target of a more 'routine' killing, hence the lack of mutilation that was the Ripper's signature.

The policemen on the scene quickly kick-started an investigation. Diemschutz and Kozebrodsky had failed to find a constable, but club member Morris Eagle, who had also seen the body, did and Constable 252H Henry Lamb came running, soon to be joined by 426H William Gunner. Like Abberline's men at the Tower three years earlier, Lamb closed the gates to Dutfield's Yard and set about taking witness statements from the club members. Twenty-eight of them were searched and some complained later about rough treatment from the police.

We have to see this in context. Four women had now died at the hands of a maniac who clearly struck where and when he liked and there was huge pressure on the police to make an arrest that would stick. Most of the club members were recently arrived Russian or Polish Jews, whose command of English was probably limited. Lamb, Gunner and the detectives who arrived later would have seen this as failing to help police with their enquiries.

Inspector Reid went to the mortuary in St-George's-in-the-East (one of the few original 'Ripper related' buildings still standing) because identification was vital. She was forty-two, he guessed (Liz Stride was actually forty-five) and had grey eyes and a damaged mouth with missing front teeth. Her clothes were old, black[1] and shabby. The dead woman had been born Elizabeth Gustafsdottir in Torslanda, Sweden, and was a registered prostitute there by the age of seventeen. In 1866 she applied for permission to emigrate to Britain, possibly to work in domestic service with a family living near Hyde Park. Three years later she married John Stride, but the coffee shop business they opened failed and both of them suffered ill health. He died of heart disease in 1884 and Liz took up with a labourer called Michael Kidney. For the rest of her life she lived on and off with him as well as in various doss houses in the area.

Abberline is oddly missing from the Liz Stride case until several days later. Reid was at the murder scene, so was Pinhorn. The most senior policeman there was Chief Inspector (acting Superintendent) John West, but he was junior to Abberline and seems to have co-ordinated the Ripper enquiries as his second-in-command. Those two would have been old comrades, since West had been with H Division since 1884. There was considerable movement in the command structure, as we have seen at Scotland Yard, but among detectives on the ground too. Reid was on leave when Annie Chapman died and it was West who specifically asked for Abberline. Just prior to Liz Stride's murder, while Arnold was away, West deputized for him, reverting to the Chief Inspector rank later.

It may be that Abberline's attention was diverted elsewhere because, less than an hour after the finding of Liz Stride's body, the Ripper struck again, in Mitre Square, in the jurisdiction of the City Police. The Met had no jurisdiction here, but both forces were clearly hunting the same man and the clue left by the killer – almost the only clue that Jack did leave throughout his spree – brought him squarely back into H Division again, pointing to the fact that Abberline was right in his belief – the Ripper was a local man.

Catherine Eddowes, the City police would later discover, was born in Wolverhampton. The family had moved to Bermondsey when she was a child and by the 1860s she was living with an ex-soldier called Thomas Conway. They had three children between

1865 and 1873 but by 1880 the common law marriage was over. She blamed his beatings. He blamed her drinking. Since 1881 Kate had been living, mostly in doss houses, with John Kelly, a quiet, inoffensive market porter. On the day before she died, the couple had returned from hop-picking in Kent (the badly-paid, back-breaking work was a poor East Ender's idea of a holiday) and they split up, probably as a financial necessity. Kelly ended up in Cooney's Lodging House in Thrawl Street while Kate went to the Shoe Lane Workhouse. She told an official there that she thought she knew the identity of the Whitechapel murderer, although this may have been an attention-grabbing story he put about later.

At 8.30pm on the night she died, Kate was picked up by City Constable 31 Louis Robinson as she slumped, drunk, in Aldgate High Street. Robinson had personal experience of this – eight months earlier he had been officially reprimanded for being drunk on duty himself. With the help of colleague Constable George Simmons he got Kate back to a cell in Bishopsgate Police Station. Having given her name as 'Nothing' she slept it off until 1am when the duty officer, Constable George Hutt, let her go. Hutt's 'Too late for you to get any more drink' was a laughable comment bearing in mind the constant availability of alcohol in the East End. The man could not know he was sending Kate Eddowes to her death, of course, but he was the sort who gave the police a bad name. He did not report information received in August 1880; was absent from his beat and lied about it two months later; was drunk on duty in July 1883 and off duty nearly two years later. The year after the Ripper case he would be suspended and allowed to resign after beating up a suspect at Moor Lane Station.

'Good night, old cock,' were Kate's last words to Hutt and she wandered away towards Mitre Square.

It was here that City Constable Edward Watkins found her body, ironically opposite a policeman's house in the darkest corner of the poorly-lit square. He had been summoned by George Morris, the night watchman at the Kearley and Tonge warehouse across the square, who shouted 'For God's sake, mate, come to assist me. There's another woman cut up to pieces.'

He was right. Police surgeon Frederick Brown of the City Police has left the most detailed description of any Ripper victim, as well as detailed drawings of the crime scene and mortuary appearance of the body. For the first time there was damage to the face – both eyelids had been nicked vertically, her nose had been severely gashed and there was a triangular cut on both cheeks like an inverted letter 'v'. One of the ear lobes was badly cut. The throat was cut across and the intestines drawn out through the abdominal mutilations. It would later be apparent in Golden Lane Mortuary that Kate's uterus and one kidney had been removed – the classic taking away of trophies by a serial killer.

If the timings of the police patrols in the area are correct, then Jack met Kate Eddowes, went with her into secluded Mitre Square, cut her throat, disembowelled her and removed her organs, all in semi-darkness and all in fifteen minutes. Various experts have doubted whether this was possible, but the police timings were never seriously challenged and the speed of the killing only added to the Ripper legend.

Laboriously the City police listed all the items on or near the body, effectively listing all Kate Eddowes's worldly goods; a bonnet, jacket, three skirts (vital if 'carrying the banner' in the autumn and winter months), a linsey bodice, petticoat, chemise and a pair of men's lace up boots. She carried several handkerchiefs, clay pipes, rags, a box of sugar, tea, a comb, a ball of hemp, a spoon, a knife and a pair of spectacles. Her apron was so dirty it appeared black, but part of it was missing.

Constable 254A Alfred Long found that. Typical of the reinforcements drafted in to Whitechapel from outlying areas, Long was from A Division in Whitehall. This was his first night on duty on the Goulston Street beat and he noticed a bloodstained apron lying near a standpipe at the entrance to Wentworth Model Buildings. It looked as though someone had used the tap and the apron to wipe blood and faeces from his hands. He also noticed what has become one of the most tiresome and confusing of all the 'clues' in the Ripper case – the chalk writing on a wall inside the entrance way that said 'The Juwes are the men that will not be blamed for nothing'. This may of course have had nothing to do with the Ripper crimes at all and, at that stage, Constable Long had no idea that a murder had been committed streets away from him.[2]

Superintendent Arnold had no doubt that the writing had no connection with the killings, but he also realized the potential implication and an anti-Semitic riot on his hands was the last thing he wanted. Petticoat Lane market, around the corner in Wentworth Street, was about to open as daylight crept over Whitechapel and Arnold had an inspector with a wet sponge and bucket standing by until Commissioner Warren could be notified and asked for his views. He agreed with Arnold and the Goulston Street graffito disappeared for ever.

The next we hear from Abberline he was interviewing two crucial witnesses in the Berner Street case. The first was another attention-seeker, the grocer Matthew Packer who ran a general store two doors down from Dutfield's Yard. When interviewed by Sergeant Stephen White of H Division, Packer (and indeed his whole family) said they had neither seen nor heard anything that night. In fact the onset of rain by about half past eleven had led them to close the shop early.[3] Two days later he was telling a very different story to Charles Le Grand and J.H. Batchelor, two private detectives hired by the Whitechapel Vigilance Committee, the *Evening News* and the *Daily Telegraph*. According to their version, Packer had sold a bunch of grapes to a man and woman fitting Liz Stride's description. Packer described the man and even remembered the brief conversation he had with him.

The two detectives, with a great deal of derring-do, whisked Packer off to the mortuary in St George's-in-the-East where he identified Liz Stride as the woman he had seen. They also found a convenient grape stem in the gateway to Dutfield's Yard, thus confirming Packer's story, and took him in a cab to see Sir Charles Warren himself.

With all this going on, Inspector Moore got wind of what the private detectives were up to and sent Sergeant White back to Packer to re-interview him. The implications were plain. Packer was telling everybody, especially the *Evening News* and the *Telegraph*, that the police had not asked him any questions, merely nosed about in his back yard. So it was left to members of the public working on behalf of the Vigilance Committee to bypass the policeman on the ground and go to the very top. It is very unlikely that Warren actually saw the three men, but either Moore or Abberline probably did. The information ended up in a report written on 4 October by Assistant Commissioner Alexander Bruce, who had personally visited the murder sites of Polly Nichols and Annie Chapman.

Packer's description of the man seen talking to Liz Stride is meaningless, as Swanson noted on 19 October. To begin with Le Grand of the Strand had a criminal record and clearly Packer was more interested in any reward that their paymasters might throw his way than in catching the Whitechapel murderer. The grape story was pure fiction, as the post mortem of Liz Stride showed – she had not eaten any grapes. So far was Packer discredited that he was not called as a witness at the inquest.[4] In the meantime, the Press cry had gone up of more police incompetence and Inspector Moore's internal enquiry into Sergeant White's investigation wasted a great deal of time. We do not know exactly where and when Abberline talked to Packer, but the meeting gives us one of the three known pen and ink sketches of him – a portly man in a dark suit and derby hat with the dundreary whiskers already rather obsolete by 1888. We can be sure that the conversation was less than cordial.

Abberline's second witness, who in the end turned out to be no more reliable, was Israel Schwartz. The man was a Hungarian Jew who lived at 22 Ellen Street, around the corner from Dutfield's Yard. Although the report on his evidence was compiled by Swanson on 4 October, it was Abberline who interviewed him and Abberline who was able to explain one of the on-going mysteries of the case. Schwartz witnessed a 'domestic' at the Dutfield Yard entrance at 12.45am. A man and woman were arguing and the man spun the woman round and threw her to the ground. She screamed, but not loudly, and Schwartz crossed the road to avoid the situation, only to see another man lighting a pipe on that side of the pavement. The assailant called out 'Lipski' and the pipe man began to follow Schwartz, who was now rather alarmed. He ran as far as a railway arch but was not pursued. He couldn't tell whether the two men knew each other or whether they were together. Schwartz told Abberline the assailant was about thirty years of age, five feet five inches tall, with a fair complexion, dark hair, small moustache, full face. He had broad shoulders and wore a dark jacket and trousers with a peaked cap. 'Pipe man' was much taller – five feet eleven inches – and was aged about thirty-five with the usual dark, shabby clothes and a clay pipe.

However, Schwartz was sure about the woman, because Abberline had him taken to the mortuary and he positively identified Liz Stride.

This incident has caused Ripperologists considerable difficulty. Some contend that the assailant *was* the Ripper and that 'pipe man' was his look-out. If he was there on the other 'nights in question' this may explain why the killer was never caught. On the other hand, where was he minutes later when Louis Diemschutz turned up with his horse and cart? We have to remember that Schwartz spoke virtually no English. When he talked to Abberline at Leman Street he had a friend with him as an interpreter. We also have to remember that a *Star* reporter muddied the waters by tracking Schwartz down and getting a slightly different story from him. In this version, it was 'pipe man' who shouted some sort of warning, as though to an assailant. Since the interpreter in both cases was the same man, clearly *somebody* got it wrong and I am inclined to believe it was the story-hungry newsman rather than the experienced police interrogator who made the mistake. To the *Star* man, Schwartz said he saw a knife in the assailant's hand, but there is no mention of that in the police report.

What are we to make of it? It is entirely possible that the man Schwartz saw attacking Stride was the Ripper, but it was equally possible that someone else found her minutes after the fracas on the pavement and killed her. Schwartz's descriptions are so vague they could cover half the men in the Abyss; only the height of 'pipe man' would have been unusual and no one else mentions anyone that tall in connection with any of the other Ripper murders.

Abberline explained 'Lipski' to his superiors at the Yard. Israel Lipski was a Jew hanged for the murder of fellow lodger Miriam Angel at 16 Batty Street (nearby) in August 1887. The term had become one of abuse for any Jew, like 'Yid'. My own opinion is that 'pipe man' and Liz Stride's attacker *did* know each other and that the assailant, seeing Schwartz approaching, called out to his 'mate' to get rid of the Jew, because he could already, from what Schwartz had seen, be charged with assault. The papers were convinced that the police did not believe Schwartz's story and certainly he did not appear as a witness at the inquest. The double event saw a re-doubling of police efforts as full-scale panic began to grip the East End. House-to-house enquiries were made the length of Berner Street. Some 80,000 leaflets were printed, linking (without names) the murders of Polly Nichols, Annie Chapman and Liz Stride. Any suspicious behaviour, especially of lodgers, should be reported to the nearest police station. The problem was that the Abyss was full of strangers, many exhibiting strange behaviour. We cannot even be certain that Jack's victims knew each other, for all they walked the same streets and probably drank in the same pubs. The common lodging houses which Abberline knew so well were visited and over 2,000 inmates interviewed. Slaughtermen were questioned because of the method of murder involved; sailors were quizzed as men who could slip in and out of the area via the Docks. In a move that would be wholly unacceptable today, Asiatics were targeted (the precise reason for this is not made clear) and among other likely foreigners, Greek gypsies were traced, as were 'cowboys' who were satisfactorily accounted for.[5]Abberline may have attended the inquest on Liz Stride, which opened under Coroner Wynne E. Baxter at the Vestry Hall, Cable Street, on 1 October, but the official 'watcher' was Edmund Reid. On the last day, Superintendent Arnold joined him. Constable Dew, who saw her in the mortuary, wrote later that 'traces of prettiness remained in her face and there must have been a time when she was exceedingly proud of her curly black hair.'

The inquest painstakingly checked the woman's last hours on the night of Saturday 29 September. She was drinking in the Queen's Head on the corner of Commercial Street and Fashion Street at 6.30pm. She was back at her doss half an hour later at 32 Flower and Dean, borrowing a clothes brush from a fellow inmate. The labourers saw her leave the Bricklayers' Arms in Settles Street with a man at 11.00pm, walking in the direction of Commercial Road. Three quarters of an hour later, labourer William Marshall saw her outside his house at 64 Berner Street with what may have been the same man. 'You would say anything but your prayers,' the man said to her and they walked off in the direction of Dutfield's Yard. The rest was mystery.

While the City Police launched their own independent inquiry into the Eddowes murder in Mitre Square, the Lord Mayor offered a

£500 reward for information leading to an arrest. Throughout the weeks that followed, the City Force did its own thing. When Robert Peel had created the Met nearly sixty years earlier, he had not included the City because they had a reasonably organized police already. Consequently, the Home Secretary did not run the City Force as he did the Met and the inevitable rivalry between the two constabularies meant that they sometimes failed to share information which could have been vital. It is true there were nightly meetings at Leman Street police station, almost certainly convened by Abberline, at which Detective Sergeant Robert Sagar represented the City Force. Swanson believed this was full cooperation, but without the over-riding control of the Home Office there remains a lingering doubt and to put a sergeant, even one as relatively erudite as Sagar, in this key role, says it all.

Neither was it all a bed of roses at the Met. In spite of the appalling Whitechapel murders – or perhaps because of them – cracks were appearing in the composure of everyone from the Home Secretary downwards. Every morning meetings were held at the Home Office between Robert Anderson, the newly-appointed Assistant Commissioner CID, James Monro, 'Dolly' Williamson, Swanson and Abberline. Other detectives were drafted in as necessary. The only senior name missing from these high-level meetings was that of the Commissioner himself and, as the fogs of October settled, Charles Warren found himself increasingly isolated and at loggerheads with everyone.

'Everyone' was bombarding the police, the Home Office and the newspapers with hundreds of pieces of well-meaning (or malicious) advice. Apart from the anonymous cranks copying the 'Dear Boss' letter by claiming to be the murderer, others offered up names of suspects from as far away as America. Advice was also given, from wearing rubber soles on police boots to sending detectives out in drag to mingle with the street walkers. Some of this was so ludicrous that Donald Swanson's team at the Yard, who usually had the task of sifting it all, could consign the missive to the nearest wastepaper basket; but some had to be followed up, just in case. And that meant that Abberline's team on the streets had to chase shadows.

One such example was that of John Davidson, who wandered into a cabman's shelter in Bayswater on the afternoon following the 'double event', claiming to be a doctor recently returned from India and to be guilty of the Whitechapel murders. He seemed to have been drinking and while chatting and eating a chop with the cab-man, signed a temperance pledge with the name J. Duncan. All credit is due to Abberline's men that they were able to trace the man, discover his real name and find he had a watertight alibi for the night in question. Another 'lunatic at large'; another red herring.

But the lunatic at large on the night of Thursday, 8 November was the real thing. Contrary to the story line in *From Hell* Inspector Abberline did not know Mary Jane Kelly, but Constable Walter Dew did. In his later memoirs he recorded that she was good-looking and usually paraded around the area with two female friends wearing a very clean white apron. Mary had so many aliases – Fair Emma, Ginger, Black Mary – that we cannot be sure that various witnesses were all talking about the same woman. Some information was gleaned quickly by Abberline's team; some of it has not come to light until recently when diligent researchers have been able to find helpful nuggets here and there. Mary was born in Limerick, Ireland, probably in 1863 and moved as a child with her family to Wales. Her father, John Kelly, worked as an iron founder in Carmarthenshire and Mary was one of a large brood. Her marriage to a collier named Davies ended in disaster after two or three years when he was killed in a mine explosion. She drifted to the relatively bright lights of Cardiff and took to the streets for a living. In London by 1884, Mary may have worked in a West End bordello (the polite euphemism the Victorians used for a brothel) and may have accompanied a rich client to France (she often styled herself Marie Jeanette).

Like much else in Mary Kelly's life, none of the above can be backed up by hard fact. An attractive young girl of twenty-one would be more likely to end up in the fashionable West End then on the dismal streets of Whitechapel, but she was certainly there by 1888 and there is no hard evidence to explain her rapid decline. Various accounts have her working for a Mrs Buki in St George's Street off the still notorious[6] Ratcliff Highway; living with a man named Morganstone; cohabiting with a builder's labourer, Joseph Fleming; and lodging with a Mrs Carthy on Breezer's Hill. By April 1887 she was living in Cooney's doss house in Thrawl Street.

Much of the information on Mary comes from Joseph Barnett, her on-off live-in lover, with whom she took up in April. Although recent writers have tried to pin the Ripper label on Barnett, he seems to have been a simple soul with a stammer, who didn't approve of Mary's lifestyle or her streetwalking friends and may have been gullible enough to believe any fanciful story she told him.

None of this would have been known to Inspector Abberline when he was called to 13 Miller's Court off Dorset Street on the day of the Lord Mayor of London's Show, Friday 9 November. Dorset Street itself had an evil reputation and was called 'Dosset' Street because of the number of common lodging houses along it. The roadway was packed with a jostling, excited crowd that by now knew the Ripper had struck again and found this infinitely more watchable that the Lord Mayor's procession. Abberline got to Miller's Court by 11.30am and forced his way through the police cordon down a narrow passageway which could only allow one person through at a time. Uniformed policemen were dotted around, as were detectives headed by Walter Beck, everyone un-decided as to how to proceed. Beck had been the inspector on duty at Commercial Street that morning and got a call shortly after 11.00am. Abberline was either at Leman Street or the Yard and it would have been his first instinct to enter the death room – a dingy twelve foot by twelve foot lodging that contained a bed, two chairs, a table and the eviscerated corpse of Mary Jane Kelly. No doubt he looked in through the broken window pane and no doubt he was as shocked and horrified as everyone else who witnessed the scene. The first to see it had been Thomas 'Indian Harry' Bowyer, who had called to collect Mary's rent arrears (she owed £1 9s) at 10.45am. He had dashed to find his boss, the landlord John McCarthy, who had come round to No. 13 to see for himself. McCarthy had then sent Bowyer to Commercial Street.

The first doctor on the scene was the long-suffering George Bagster Phillips, who was all too familiar with Jack's work by now. Having satisfied himself by looking at the corpse on the bed that Mary was 'not in need of any immediate attention from me'[7] he suggested the crime scene remained undisturbed until senior officers arrived. The dithering by Beck, Phillips and now Abberline has been criticized by several writers who believe that nearly three hours were lost and the trail of the killer was beginning to cool. In fact, whether intentionally or not, Phillips and the detectives were actually preserving a crime scene. The murder sites of Martha Tabram, Polly Nichols, Annie Chapman, Liz Stride and Kate Eddowes had been hopelessly compromised, to use modern jargon, by the size elevens of umpteen policemen, nosy neighbours and passers-by. Number 13 Miller's Court would be different. Although no fingerprint evidence would be taken (that technology lay three years in the future in 1888), photographs of an undisturbed crime scene were. These were unique in the annals of the Ripper investigation and they showed Mary Kelly and her little room in exactly the state that Jack had left them.

Beck had told Abberline that bloodhounds had been sent for and this, although controversial, was probably the best technical hope the police had of tracking the killer. The dogs concerned, Barnaby and Burgho, had been lent by Edwin Brough of Scarborough as some of the finest trackers in the country. They had been tried out in Hyde Park a month earlier but city streets defeated them; Mr Brough's asking price for the animals was obscene and they had been sent back. So on the morning of 9 November, there were in fact no dogs available.

By 1.20pm, while the crowd in Dorset Street became ever more fractious and demanded to know what was going on, Superintendent Arnold arrived to say no dogs were coming and the investigation had better start. The delay came about in fact because, under intense pressure from all sides, Commissioner Warren had chosen the previous day to resign and the Yard was, temporarily, leaderless. The locked door of No. 13 was forced (the key had been lost sometime earlier, but those in the know could unlock it by putting their hand through the missing window pane). While Phillips concentrated on the appalling wounds to Mary Kelly's body, Abberline made a careful inventory of the room. It was so small that the door, opening to the right, bumped against one of the tables. To Abberline's left were two windows, both curtained, one with the broken pane. There was another, smaller, table, once a washstand, in front of the furthest window and straight ahead, a fireplace and to its left, a cupboard. The bed on which the body lay was in the corner against a wooden partition which cut the room off from the rest of No. 26, a three-storey building. Over the fireplace, in a desperate attempt by Mary herself or her landlord to make the hovel a home was a print, 'The Fisherman's Widow', and the wallpaper was now so filthy (part of it daubed with blood splashes of course) that the pattern had vanished.

No doubt Abberline took careful notice of the dead body, but he could leave that to experts like Bagster Phillips. He was not to know that the doctor's report would be woefully brief, that the coroner would cut the inquest short or that the detailed description of the corpse by Dr Thomas Bond of A Division would be lost until 1987 when an anonymous someone returned it to Scotland Yard. She still had the remains of a chemise (petticoat) but so little of this was left intact that Bond missed it in his report. She was lying in the middle of the bed with her head turned to the left, looking, as it were, towards the door. Her legs were wide apart and her abdomen had been ripped open, all the viscera removed. Her breasts had been cut off and one of them was found under the body. Other organs were draped on the table by the bed. Her face was gashed beyond all recognition, the throat had been cut through and large pieces of flesh had been hacked from the legs. Most macabre of all, the heart was missing.

Such was the furore over this latest and most ghastly murder that anybody who was anybody turned up. Bond was sent for by Robert Anderson who, according to some accounts, came along in person to see for himself. Bond brought his assistant Dr Charles Hebbert and Drs Gordon Brown and John Gabe also arrived. At some point during the afternoon a police photographer took at least three photographs; one of the exterior of 13 Miller's Court showing the door and windows; another from the door showing Mary's body on the bed; and a third from behind the bed (it is not clear quite how this was taken) showing the viscera on the side table. In terms of compromising the crime scene, we now have a *minimum* of six people in that room – Abberline, Phillips, Bond, Hebbert, Gabe and the photographer certainly and very likely Beck, Anderson, perhaps Inspector Reid and assorted constables. Had the killer left any footprints in Mary's blood which must have been all over the floor, there was precious little chance of finding them after that.

It may well have been because of this overcrowding that Abberline decided to return the next day to complete his search of the room. At about 4.00pm, a tarpaulin-covered horse-drawn wagon drew up outside the narrow entrance to Miller's Court (Dorset Street had by now been cleared of ghouls with a police cordon at both ends) and Mary Kelly's body was taken away. Either Abberline or Arnold instigated a house-to-house search of the area, finding witnesses and collecting statements. What intrigued Abberline was the fireplace. A fire had recently been lit there and there were portions of female clothing, including a hat, in the ashes in the grate. The heat had been so fierce that the kettle spout had melted. Abberline gave his opinion at the subsequent inquest that he believed the killer lit the fire to give him light to carry out his mutilations. Most subsequent writers have rubbished this, stating that clothes would smoulder rather than burn brightly. But what if the Ripper put something else on the fire, something that would produce intense heat and light, if only for a few minutes? Experimental archaeologists and scientists looking at the way a human body burns have carried out experiments on pigs. Melting body parts produces a fierce incandescence. In the confined space of the grate in Mary Kelly's room, with clothing to act as a wick, who is to say – although Abberline did not – that such a heat was created by Mary Kelly's burning heart? Those who maintain that the heart is difficult to burn are just plain wrong.

Many witnesses were quizzed by detectives in the days following the murder. The first and of greatest interest to Abberline was Joseph Barnett and he tackled him personally, even though virtually all the witness statements taken by other officers are in Abberline's handwriting. If Barnett seriously crossed the Inspector's mind as a suspect, it can't have been for long. The fact that Mary Kelly was at least twenty years younger than the other Ripper victims and that she was killed indoors has given some researchers reason to believe that she was not a Ripper victim. To Abberline and anybody with the forensic facts at their disposal, it was obvious that she was; in fact she represented the apogee of his work. If Barnett had killed Mary, he must therefore have killed the others as well and this hypothesis simply did not hold water.

Barnett had met Mary on Good Friday (April 8) 1887 and they lived together at a variety of addresses. He lost his job at Billingsgate Fish Market in July 1888, perhaps for theft. He quarrelled with Mary on 30 October, probably over the arrival of another prostitute to share the room at Miller's Court, and went to lodge at Buller's boarding house in Bishopsgate. He seems to have been genuinely fond of Mary, seeing her almost every day and giving her money (although the source of his income is unknown). On the night of the murder, Barnett visited No. 13 and found Mary talking to another prostitute from Miller's Court, who may have been Lizzie Albrook or Maria Harvey. He left amicably at about 8.00pm and went back to his lodging. The coroner at the inquest praised Barnett for his eloquent delivery, which may be because he suffered from echolalia – compulsive repetition of phrases said to him. Abberline grilled the man for four hours and had his clothes checked for bloodstains. Joe Barnett was in the clear. But George Hutchinson was not. Of all the witnesses in the Whitechapel murders, the groom-turned-labourer George Hutchinson stands out as perhaps the oddest. He was not called to the inquest because at that time nobody knew he existed. At 6.00pm on the evening of 12 November Hutchinson volunteered himself at Commercial Street Station and was inter-viewed by Abberline, whose report still survives. The inspector believed Hutchinson's story, that the labourer had known Mary Kelly for about three years and occasionally gave her 'a few shillings'. Since she tried to cadge money off him on the day she died, this seems to have been a regular occurrence. Hutchinson did not admit that he got anything in exchange for the cash, but it seems at least likely. He lived at the Victoria Home, a lodging house in Commercial Street only yards from Miller's Court, and had been out of work for several weeks by the time of the murder.

At about 2.00am in the morning of 9 November, Hutchinson was passing Flower and Dean Street, possibly on his way home, when Mary Kelly stopped him and asked him to lend her sixpence. He told her he was broke and she walked off in search of cash, heading in the direction of Thrawl Street. Hutchinson saw a man stop her, tap her on the shoulder and talk to her. They burst out laughing. She said 'Alright', and he said, 'You will be alright for what I have told you,' (possibly the fee for her services). He put his right arm around her and off they went. Hutchinson was alarmed. The whole area was on the alert, with regular police and vigilance committee patrols, even though there had been no attacks for nearly six weeks. Mary Kelly was vulnerable. Although Hutchinson doesn't mention it, others do; she had been drinking and may not have had the usual careful reactions she might have shown when sober. Hutchinson stood outside the Queen's Head on the corner of Commercial and Fashion Streets and stooped to look at the man's face, letting him know he had seen him. The stranger glared back and the pair walked off towards Dorset Street.

Hutchinson followed them and watched them loitering at the entrance to Miller's Court for about three minutes. He heard Mary say, 'Alright, my dear, come along, you will be comfortable.' He placed his arm on her shoulder and kissed her. She told him she had lost her handkerchief and he produced a red one. Then they vanished into the Court.

Hutchinson waited for forty-five minutes (it would be about 3.00am by now) and since the stranger had not reappeared, Hutchinson gave up and went home. He was almost certainly the man seen hanging around by Sarah Lewis, a 'laundress' of Great Pearl Street, whom Abberline also questioned around this time.

What stands out about Hutchinson is the extraordinarily detailed description of the man he saw with Mary. Most of us make dreadful eye-witnesses. We are not sharply observant and bad light and dodgy memory play tricks on us. Not so Hutchinson! The stranger was thirty-four or thirty-five years old, with a pale complexion and dark eyes. His hair was dark with a curled moustache and he had a surly appearance (possibly because he knew Hutchinson was watching him). His coat was long and dark with astrakhan trim to collar and cuffs and he had button boots and gaiters with a heavy gold watch chain, a horse shoe tie pin and he walked 'very sharp' (fast). Hutchinson said the man was Jewish and he would know him again.

Abberline sent two of his men around the streets of Whitechapel with Hutchinson in case he should spot him. Aficionados of the top-hatted, gentleman killer slumming it in the East End have seized on Hutchinson's description because the clothes indicate someone who is rich. What Abberline made of it we do not know. Around ninety percent of the men in the area were Jewish and no doubt some of them frequented prostitutes; but if Hutchinson's man was Jack, the timing does not make sense. The police surgeons estimated the time of death of Mary Kelly as between 4.00 and 5.45am. This meant that the Jewish gentleman would have stayed with Mary for nearly two hours before killing her. Much more likely is the scenario that Hutchinson's suspect went on his way, light of a few coppers, and Mary went out one last time to augment her income. Hutchinson's intensely detailed description – he even mentions the man's eyelashes – may mean he was describing someone he knew, disliked and wanted to put in the frame for murder. Crime writer John Eddleston believes that this was a blind and that Hutchinson himself was Jack. Whoever he was, Mary's client took his handkerchief away with him. The only artefact Abberline found in Mary's room was Joe Barnett's clay pipe. Before he interviewed Hutchinson, Abberline was still keeping an open mind and was doggedly pursuing his enquires. On 6 December, a reporter from the *Morning Advertiser* saw the Inspector pick up a suspect in a 'strongly escorted' cab and whisk him off to Leman Street. Abberline muttered to one of his men – 'Keep this quiet; we have got the right man at last. This is a big thing.'[8]

The 'big thing' was another lunatic, a Polish Jew named Joseph Isaacs. It may be that Abberline had received a tip-off and, if so, it was wide of the mark. Isaacs was behaving oddly in the days before the Kelly murder, threatening women verbally and leaving behind a violin bow at his lodgings in Little Pasternoster Row off Dorset Street. Three days after Mary Kelly died, he was sent down for twenty-one days at Barnet Police Court for theft. On the day of his release, 5 December, he collected his violin bow and robbed a jeweller's shop before being arrested by Detective Sergeant William Record, who took him to Bow Street. The newspaper account of his arrest refers to an attack on prostitute Annie Farmer on 21 November, but Isaacs could not have been responsible for that; he was in gaol at the time. Exactly what Abberline thought he had on him is unknown.

Once again, dozens of arrests, gallons of ink, miles of shoe leather worn. Once again, brick walls, unshakeable alibis and still more criticism of the police. And it was all costing an arm and a leg.

Monro desperately defended it to the Home Office on 7 December. One inspector, nine sergeants and 126 constables had been deployed in plain clothes to patrol the killing fields. 'The expense will be considerable, amounting to about £5 per diem; but it is, in my opinion, justifiable and should be incurred.'[9]

And in the aftermath of the Kelly murder, almost as suddenly as Inspector Abberline was drafted into the Whitechapel case, he was drafted out. And we don't know why.

Chapter 8

The Diaries of G.F. Abberline

The story of the hunt for the Whitechapel murderer is complex enough without the royal connection and although this part of Abberline's story more properly belongs in Chapter 1 of this work, I include it here because it was once seriously proposed as fact.

Ask anyone on the Clapham omnibus today who Jack the Ripper was and they will tell you it was probably the queen's doctor and the whole thing was hushed up because it involved 'the highest in the land'.

This was the conspiracy theory hatched by journalist Stephen Knight in 1976 in his book *Jack the Ripper: the Final Solution*. It was nothing of the sort, of course, but with its intrigue in court circles and its involvement of senior royals, it caught the public's imagination as no other book on the subject had before or has since. Knight's informant was Joseph Gorman-Sickert, who claimed to be the illegitimate son of the Victorian artist Walter Sickert and Alice Crook, who was herself, Sickert junior claimed, the daughter of shopgirl Annie Crook and Prince Albert Victor, grandson of Queen Victoria and heir to the throne.

So far, so unlikely, but how does it all tie in with the Ripper murders? The story, which was the core of at least three movies on the Whitechapel killings, goes like this. Walter Sickert worked in a studio in Cleveland Street and across the road stood a flower shop where Annie Crook worked. Since Sickert was hired to cultivate the prince's artistic interests, Albert Victor, the Duke of Clarence, was a frequent visitor and met and fell in love with Annie. Ignoring her humble birth and Catholic faith, Clarence married the girl and they had a daughter – Joseph Sickert's mother, Alice. According to Stephen Knight, drawing on the incidents of clashes between the police and the people in Trafalgar Square on 'Bloody Sunday' 1887, the whole country teetered on the brink of anarchy and had this marriage/child scandal become known, the royal family would have collapsed and Britain with it. A distraught Victoria turned to her confidant, her physician-in-ordinary Sir William Gull, and asked him to help. A similar request was made to the doctor by Lord Salisbury, the Prime Minister, a fellow Mason and someone who could be relied upon to defend his own status quo at all costs.

Unfortunately for all concerned, word of the marriage had already got out because a witness to the ceremony was Mary Kelly and she told a few close friends – Polly Nichols, Annie Chapman, Liz Stride and Kate Eddowes. With surgical precision, Gull set about eliminating these women. He did not, of course, know what they looked like or where to find them and this is where Walter Sickert came in. He knew Annie, he knew Mary and may well have known the others too. He acted as chief scout and look-out man while Gull, increasingly deranged by 1888, was taken to the Abyss in a coach driven by John Netley. One by one, he beckoned the victims into the coach, killed and mutilated them in Masonic tradition, with cut throats and ripped-out intestines, and Netley dumped the bodies where they were found. The murders ended with Mary Kelly because she was the last of them 'in the know'.

As for Clarence, he was separated from his darling Annie forever. Gull had the woman removed to his private sanatorium and operated on her brain so that her memory was impaired. Alice lived on (to become Joseph Sickert's mother), but not before John Netley had tried twice to run her down with his coach, finally killing himself in the process. Gull died, hopelessly insane, the year after the murders, but his coffin was found to contain stones so that the actual date of his death – and burial place – is unknown.

It is difficult to know where to start to demolish this cavalcade of nonsense. 'Bloody Sunday' was indeed an unsettling incident, but it was not the first time, nor the last, that some people claimed the country was on the verge of collapse.[1] The queen had been unpopular in the 1860s because of her grief-stricken reclusiveness after the death of Prince Albert; by 1887 she was the focus of her own Golden Jubilee and had even ridden through a star-struck Whitechapel, everybody madly waving their Union Flags. There is no evidence that Sickert had a studio in Cleveland Street or that Clarence ever went near the place. There is no record of a marriage between him and anyone; no proof of the parenthood of Alice Crook. Gull was not a Mason, so the link with Salisbury breaks down. Neither were the victims killed according to Masonic ritual – merely the far more arcane and personal ritual of a serial killer. Even if everything Sickert told Knight were true, are we seriously to believe that the government of the greatest power on earth could not merely buy the silence of a few street women, rather than going to the extremes of murder? Most damning of all, William Withey Gull was seventy-two at the time of the Whitechapel murders and had suffered two strokes. He was physically incapable of wielding a knife. And all Jack's victims died where they were found – there was no black-draped, sepulchral coach creaking eerily through the Whitechapel night. If there had been, someone in those surprisingly busy streets would have seen it and commented on the fact.

The highest in the land theory may have been nonsense, but it must have made Stephen Knight a wealthy man in the brief time he had left. A year after publication, he suffered an epileptic fit and a cerebral tumour was discovered. He wrote his last book, *The Brotherhood*, an exposé of the 'evils' of freemasonry, in 1985 and died after a failed brain operation two years later.

But one strand of the story that Knight did not include in *Final Solution* was one taken up by Melvyn Fairclough in 1991. Fairclough was a friend of Joseph Sickert and went into print on his behalf in *The Ripper and the Royals*. Sickert's foreword to the book claimed that Knight had misinterpreted the material Sickert had given him and that the *Final Solution*, though broadly accurate, had been 'wrong on many points' and 'missed out many vital details'. In the 1992 Duckworth paperback edition, this foreword is prefixed by a photocopy of a letter on Metropolitan Police paper. It is written to G.F. Goschen, in 1888 Chancellor of the Exchequer under Lord Salisbury, and is signed 'Yours respectfully, D I F G Abberline'.[2]

When Fairclough began talking to Joseph Sickert in 1984, he was shown six notebooks, three of which were written, he was told, by Inspector Abberline. Sickert's tale was that Abberline was a friend of Joseph's father, Walter, and he often visited the family in

Drummond Street. The then three-year-old remembered the detective with fondness. He smelt of tobacco:

> He was chubby and had a white moustache and underneath it you could see his shiny white teeth. His hair was white too but he was bald. He wore a bowler hat. We called him Freddy. He was very gentle. He was a lovely man.

On the occasion of his last visit, some time in 1928, Abberline gave Sickert senior his diaries. There were three books, all leather-bound; two were black with ruled pages and one was a maroon-coloured Charles Letts diary for 1896. In it, Abberline mentions people well known to Stephen Knight: William Gull; John Netley; J.K. Stephen, Clarence's tutor. But there is another name – Lord Randolph Churchill, the 'candlestick maker'.

Along with the notebooks was another with the faded, handwritten title:

Extracts
Fr........y
Exposed

This was a reference to an 1827 book, *Freemasonry Exposed*, written by an American insider, William Morgan. Fairclough writes that Abberline knew of the Masonic mutilations on the Ripper's victims and was following up the lead accordingly. The Letts section of the Abberline diaries is dated 1903 and has the words 'to be kept apart' for 18–20 May. The other diaries, bound with wax and therefore 'locked' were written between 1892 (when Abberline left the Met) and 1915.

An undated entry in the diary reads:

> Saw Walter [Sickert] with E [Eddie, the Duke of Clarence] in Spitalfields, Feb. 1887. I asked why they were there, but E told me to mind my own business. I reported this. Told to keep an eye on E and Captain G H [George Holford, Eddie's Equerry]. Later transferred to A Div.

Abberline confided to the elder Sickert that his new duties included 'minding' Eddie when he was in London. The inference was that the young man was impetuous and easily led. Abberline's job was to keep him on the straight and narrow, one at which he abysmally failed if we believe the diaries.

We know from official sources that Abberline was very closely involved in the investigation of Mary Kelly's death and the 1892 diary records a report from her landlord, John McCarthy. He had received an inexplicable postcard from Scotland which said: 'Now we've done the fourth one [sic. Kelly was the fifth of the 'canonical five']³ we shall go for the mother and daughter.'

This of course follows the convention of the 'highest in the land' theory – Annie and her daughter Alice must be taken care of, permanently.

McCarthy, says Fairclough, handed the postcard to the police and Abberline's subsequent inquiries unearthed the fact that it was likely that the postcard was sent by William Gull himself from his country house at Killiecrankie. This postcard, along with many other Whitechapel murders papers, is now missing from the official file.

A vital element in Joseph Sickert's involvement of Abberline is the role played by James Kenneth Stephen (spelt with a 'v' in the diaries). Stephen was a brilliant academic who had been Eddie's tutor at Cambridge University in 1883. He was hit on the head three years later in a freak accident and the resulting brain damage led to his death in 1892. Researcher Michael Harrison's theory, proposed in his 1972 biography of Clarence, was that the prince and his tutor were lovers and when Clarence jilted him for reasons of state, he exacted revenge on women accordingly.

The Sickert-Fairclough take on all this, based on Abberline's diaries, is that Stephen went to the inspector since he had been, as a result of his relationship with Eddie, caught up in a conspiracy to murder by the fanatical Lord Randolph Churchill, really the prime mover in the whole sordid business. Churchill, father of the far more famous Winston, was the sixth son of the Duke of Marlborough and a prominent Conservative politician. Always a man of arrogance and impetuosity, he had resigned his Cabinet post in 1886, probably hoping it would not be accepted. It was. Churchill becomes the central figure in the Abberline diaries, a man whose mind was deteriorating because of the effects of syphilis, from which he died in 1895. He was a Mason and a friend of William Gull's and when

Winston became Home Secretary in 1909 he was able to remove all police reference to his father from the official files. The allegations become ever more preposterous. Abberline knew Eddie, Alice, all about the marriage and, when Eddie heard of Churchill's plot to destroy his illicit little family, he suggested it was Victoria who should be killed. 'Who?' Abberline quotes Churchill as saying, 'The great whore herself?'

Abberline's dilemma, the diaries tell us, was that he suspected his own superiors at the Yard, Charles Warren and Robert Anderson, as high-ranking Masons, of being in on the plot. Their reticence in working with the Press was not a deliberate matter of professional policy on their part, but because they had personal reasons to keep everything under wraps. The diary mentions two occasions on which Abberline was called to a crime scene where he felt his life to be in danger. This was 1892, shortly before Abberline retired and the Ripper case closed. Abberline told Anderson that he had written down all he knew on the killings and, straight out of a crime novel, he had stashed it in a secret place to be opened in the event of his death.

When Abberline entered Mary Kelly's room in Miller's Court he found an old letter which seemed to have no link to her at all. Sharing the address on the missive with Sickert, the artist told Abberline that it probably dated to about 1690. Melvyn Fairclough had the paper checked by the British Museum who agreed it was late seventeenth century. Fairclough's industry turned up the fact that the Ship tavern in Bartholomew Lane was used for Masonic meetings and that this therefore fits with the three men Abberline's diary says were complicit in the Kelly murder:

> JK [Stephen] said the three men in room 13 were LRC [Churchill] – WWG [Gull] and – JCN [Netley]. Churchill was the ringleader and master mason, Netley the coach driver and Gull the actual murderer. Abberline believed that the scrap of paper had been dropped by Churchill because he 'had access to private libraries'[!]

Other papers Abberline found in Room 13 linked Mary, via the Bellord Domestic Agency, to domestic work with a respectable family in Cleveland Street. And he also has comments to make on the 'locked room' mystery and the fire in the grate. The reason for the delay in entering was due to the fact that a heavy washstand with marble top was blocking the door from the inside. Melvyn Fairclough believes that the second police photograph, taken from behind Mary's bed and showing her intestines on the table, actually shows the top of the marble washstand. The three killers, having done the deed, all escaped through the window. 'There is,' wrote Fairclough, 'no other explanation.'

One of the murderers, Abberline told Walter Sickert, had used a fork in the dead woman's room to handle various body parts, rather than getting blood over his hands, and those marks were clear on the kidneys for example. The fire in the grate was necessary to burn the men's clothes to avoid detection. Abberline himself removed the Kelly papers from the file as added insurance against the unpremeditated action of his superiors.

Abberline's investigation into Mary Kelly herself revealed that she had two children; one was adopted; the other sent 'by the convent' (possibly the Providence Row Night Refuge in Crispin Street) to Canada to begin a new life. These details were added in biographical thumb-nail sketches by Abberline and appear as Appendix 7 in Fairclough's book. The implication is that all the women except Catherine Eddowes knew each other, underscoring the marriage/ Alice link and explaining that the woman in Mitre Square was killed by mistake.

With the death of J.K. Stephen in 1892, Abberline decided to turn his spotlight on John Netley. He obtained a photograph of the man which he subsequently gave to Sickert and Fairclough reproduced it in his own book. Joseph Sickert maintained that the coachman was bisexual and worked as a male prostitute among polite society in the West End and had taken Eddie for his clandestine meetings with Annie Crook in Cleveland Street. The diaries imply that it was Abberline's net closing in on him that led to Netley's attempted suicide by throwing himself into the Thames on 6 February 1892. The *Observer* reported, 'A respectably dressed young man took off his boots and coat and hid them under a seat in the waiting room [of Westminster Pier] and swam a few yards.' He was rescued, struggling and gave his name as Nickley. The stashing of his boots and clothes, Fairclough contends, is not the work of a true suicide and this was Netley's attempt to fake his own death. He would 'disappear' somewhere along the Embankment and retrieve his clothes later. It was not until 1903 (as the diary states) that Abberline realized that Netley had survived and did not die until that year. The cryptic comment, written in 1915, reads 'JC Netley murdered under his own coach. Payment for Alice?'[4]

The diary contends that Netley and a petty crook, Frederico Alberici (known as 'Fingers Freddie') had murdered prostitute Emma Smith in April 1888 in their search for the women who had to be silenced. Abberline believed that Smith and Kelly were friends and that both men were working for Churchill.

On page 96 of the 1896 diary is the even more cryptic phrase – 'Butcher, Baker, Candlestick Maker'. Fairclough explains that the Butcher, clearly, was Gull, the man with the medical and Masonic connections. The Baker was variously Warren, Anderson and J.K. Stephen, part of the conspiracy, orchestrating and covering tracks. The Candlestick Maker was Churchill – the C for the family name and the M for Marlborough.

The most bizarre of all the Abberline pages is the letter addressed to George Goschen. It is written on Met stationery and in the margin is the file number 52983 which is identical to Abberline's report on Kelly in the Public Record Office. Goschen was a friend of Churchill's in the Conservative Party and took over his role when Churchill resigned. The letter read:

Sir,
With respect reference to your last instruction my interview with JK Stephen, Lord Randolf [sic] Spencer Churchill, Sir W Gull confirmed. I am sending this report for you [sic] personal attention. No further investigation will be made. I leave this in your hand. I have done our duty. Rest of my report will be sent on. I shall heed to my burns.

Fairclough believes that this is confirmation that Stephen had 'fingered' Churchill and Gull as the Whitechapel murderers. The implication is that Goschen had asked Abberline to talk to Stephen, although precisely why is unknown.

Where do we start? The most famous diary in the Ripper story is that purported to be written by murder victim James Maybrick. The convolutions of that tale are too tortuous to include here, but, in a nutshell, the Maybrick diary emerged in May 1991 in the possession of house-husband Michael Barrett, who had been given it by a friend, Tony Devereux, now dead. A number of specialist consultants were brought in by the literary agency trying to turn the potential bombshell into a book and their brief was to establish the diary's authenticity. As is usually the case with experts, they failed to agree and two camps developed – one convinced that the Liverpool cotton merchant Maybrick was the Ripper and the other that the whole thing was a hoax. Even when Barrett confessed he had forged it, the furore continued because the next day his solicitors withdrew his confession because Barrett 'was not in full control of his faculties when he made the statement.'[5]

Whatever the technical difficulties of deciding the age of ink and exactly when it is applied to paper, the fact that the diary makes twenty-four errors that would not have been made by someone writing in 1888 and that the handwriting does not match Maybrick's signature blow the authenticity of the diary out of the water.

The Abberline diaries have not been subjected to any scientific tests at all and the interpretation of them is largely Melvyn Fairclough's. Even Stephen Knight admitted that Joseph Sickert was vague and unreliable, but admits that he became caught up in the fascination of the man's story; Melvyn Fairclough likewise. To begin with, the handwriting in the diaries is clearly not Abberline's. Fairclough obtained the *Reminiscences* (which *are* genuine) and compared the handwriting and found them identical, allowing for the fact that the diaries were compiled in old age and that failing eyesight and weakening muscles can lead to slight changes. But the *Reminiscences* were written at exactly the same time as the diary, so this fails to convince. The whole tenor of the diary rests on the discredited Masonic connection and the ludicrous conspiracy theory of the 'highest in the land'. Everything about it screams fiction. The cryptic comments of 'Butcher, Baker, Candlestick Maker' are evidence, Fairclough says, of Abberline having a 'penchant for the poetic and allusive', but no one else comments on that and the diary is the sole evidence for it. The involvement of Goschen and the peculiar reference to 'burns' is incomprehensible. As for the idea that three large men (Gull in particular was a heavy seventy-two-year-old) climbed out of the tiny window at 13 Miller's Court, it is laughable.

Where are the diaries now? No one knows, although respected Ripper expert Paul Begg believes that Joseph Sickert destroyed them. And if they are forgeries, who forged them? Again, Begg does not believe that Sickert did. In his discussion with the man, who died in 2003, it was clear that Sickert himself believed totally in their authenticity. When Melvyn Fairclough first saw them in the 1990s, they were as he describes them in his book, which contains photographs of the diaries themselves.

Two things remain. The Bible of Ripperology, the *A–Z*, says in its latest edition:

> No part of Joseph Gorman-Sickert's story as allegedly told him by Walter Sickert, has ever been substantiated by concrete evidence and many details of Stephen Knight's representation of the story have been conclusively disproved.

The other problem is even more damning. Whoever forged the Abberline diaries, which reproduce errors made in an article in a 1989 issue of *True Detective*, got the inspector's initials the wrong way round in a supposed signature. 'F.G.', for 'Frederick George', unaccountably becomes 'GF'.

Chapter 9

'Jack the Ripper ... at last!'

At Wandsworth Prison on 7 April 1903, William Billington and his assistant Henry Pierrepoint hanged Severino Klosowski, otherwise known as George Chapman, for the murders of Mary Spink, Elizabeth Taylor and Maud Marsh.

Klosowski was the son of a carpenter from Nagornak, Poland who became a medical student and eventually a *feldscher* or assistant surgeon in Praga in 1897. Exactly why he moved to England in July of that year remains a mystery. Possibly his later murderous tendencies had already resulted in a homicide, or perhaps the fact that he spoke Yiddish led to anti-Semitic attacks on him. Whatever the reason he accepted a far more lowly status in London, working as a hairdresser/barber at various places in the East End before running the White Hart pub on the corner of Whitechapel High Street and George Yard.

A powerful-looking man with deep set, dark eyes and an enormous 'handlebar' moustache, Klosowski seems to have exerted mesmeric control over women. His first known conquest was Lucy Baderski, whom he may have married in October 1889. The couple moved several times over the next two years, during which a son, Wohystaw, was born and died and they ended up in Jersey City, USA. Perhaps Klosowski beat his wife or she may have missed her family, but for some reason, Lucy returned alone and pregnant in February 1892. She gave birth to a daughter, Cecilia, in May. Klosowski followed her back to London briefly in June, then disappeared.

By 1893 he was cutting people's hair in Tottenham and tried to set up a ménage-à-trois with Annie Chapman (no relation to the Ripper victim in Hanbury Street). She left him and Klosowski started using her surname as his and posing as an American. By

1895 he had taken up with Mary Spink and the pair lived in Hastings briefly before he became landlord of the Prince of Wales pub in Bartholomew Square off the City Road. There, Mary Spink died, it would later turn out, of poison by tartar emetic. A fatal dose would have been 15 grains; Mary swallowed 400. The official cause of death, on Christmas Day 1897, was phthisis (tuberculosis).

Four months later Chapman took on a new barmaid, Elizabeth Taylor, known to everyone as Bessie. Perhaps because of the speed of their relationship so soon after Mary's death, the couple moved to Bishop's Stortford to run the Grapes there. Back in London by March 1899, Chapman was now running the Monument in Southwark, south of the river. On 13 February 1901, Bessie died, according to Dr Stoker, of intestinal obstruction. In August, Maud Marsh took up Chapman's offer of a barmaid job and Chapman married her in September.

Chapman's roving eye fell on a new girl, Florence Rayner, and even though she turned down his offer of elopement to the States, Chapman had decided his relationship with Maud was over and he began feeding her poison. He must have panicked when her sister, Mrs Morris, had Maud taken to Guy's Hospital at the end of July 1902, especially when the woman recovered and was released on 20 August. Back with Chapman, however, her mysterious illness reappeared and she died on 22 October.

The policeman who arrested Chapman was Inspector George Godley, a detective sergeant at the time of the Ripper killings and the man who, in film fiction, is Abberline's 'sidekick'. But the link is not as simple as that. When Hargrave L. Adam wrote the introduction to Chapman's trial[1] in 1931 he had Godley's help and the inspector quotes Abberline as saying to him, 'I see you've caught Jack the Ripper at last.'

We have no way of knowing what the relationship between Abberline and Godley was. By 1903, Abberline had been gone from the Met for eleven years and may well have lost touch with many of his former fellow officers. In 1888, as we have seen, Godley was in J Division (Bethnal Green) and attended the inquest on Polly Nichols along with Abberline, Inspector Helson and Sergeant Enright. By this time of course Abberline was at the Yard, so it is most unlikely that he had come across Godley before. The only time his name is mentioned in the Ripper case is his following up leads given by Polly's friend, Mary Anne Connelly, known as 'Pearly Poll'. So where did Abberline's false congratulation come from? He had been drawn to talk to the Press once before. In May 1892, free of the censorship imposed on serving officers, Abberline talked to a journalist from *Cassell's Saturday Journal*. As well as expanding on the Chief Inspector's years of experience and dedication to duty, the article said:

> and it happened frequently, too, that, just as he was going to bed, he would be summoned back to the East End by a tele-graph, there to interrogate some lunatic or suspected person whom the inspector in charge would not take the responsibility of questioning. 'Theories!' exclaims the inspector, when con-versing about the murders – 'we were almost lost in theories; there were so many of them.'[2]

By 1903 Abberline was developing a new theory of his own. The arrest and subsequent trial of Klosowski/Chapman was extremely high profile. A foreigner who looked like the villain in Victorian 'penny dreadfuls' – *three* counts of murder by dastardly poisoning. Inevitably it brought the East End, where Chapman had lived, into sharp focus again. And some people were beginning to wonder whether there was any link between *this* killer and the elusive Jack of fifteen years before. One who did was ex-Superintendent Arthur Neil, who investigated the Chapman case. He was not directly involved in the Ripper enquiry, as he only joined the Met in May 1888, but he shared Abberline's view of Chapman and went into print in 1932.[3]

> We were never able to secure definite proof that Chapman was the 'Ripper' but the strong theory remains just the same. No one who had not been trained as a surgeon and a medical man could have committed the 'Ripper' crimes. As we discovered, Chapman had been a surgeon in Poland and would therefore be the only possible fiend capable of putting such knowledge to use against humanity instead of for it.

It is a huge leap of logic on Neil's part to claim that, in an area of half a million people, Chapman was the 'only possible fiend', but it does illustrate how woefully wide of the mark even experienced detectives were in their search for a man like Jack. By the time Neil's book was published, Hargrave Adam had written his account of the Chapman trial and, with it, Abberline's assertion back in 1903.

On 23 March of that year, while Chapman waited for execution at Wandsworth, a reporter of the *Pall Mall Gazette* wrote up the interview he had had with Abberline.

> Should Klosowski, the wretched man now lying under sentence of death for wife-poisoning, go to the scaffold without a 'last dying speech and confession', a great mystery forever remains unsolved but the conviction that 'Chapman' and 'Jack the Ripper' were one and the same person will not in the least be weakened in the mind of the man who is, perhaps, better qualified than anyone else in this country to express an opinion in the matter. We allude to Mr F.G. Abberline, formerly Chief Inspector of Scotland Yard ...[4]

Abberline had been following the Chapman case avidly (no doubt for old time's sake) and had been on the point of writing to Melville Macnaghten, Assistant Commissioner of the Met, but he had hurt his hand in a fall in the garden and the arrival of the *Pall Mall Gazette* man had saved him the trouble. Abberline was surrounded by press cuttings on the case and had already covered a page and a half of foolscap with his observations. The newspaperman reported that Abberline was struck by the coincidences between the Chapman murders and the Whitechapel killings:

> everything fits in and dovetails so well that I cannot help feeling that this is the man we struggled so hard to capture fifteen years ago ... there are a score of things which make one believe that Chapman is the man; and you must understand that we have never believed all those stories about Jack the Ripper being dead, or that he was a lunatic or anything of that kind.[5]

All this is music to the ears of writer R. Michael Gordon, who is convinced that Chapman was the Whitechapel murderer. What greater validation could there be for his theory than to be backed by the man who led the hunt for the Ripper on the ground? Unfortunately, Abberline was wrong, as at least two experts on the Whitechapel killings pointed out at the time.

The first was the journalist, author and playwright George R. Sims, who wrote as 'Dagonet' in *The Referee* and went into print the week after the *Pall Mall Gazette*'s article.

> It is perfectly well known at Scotland Yard who 'Jack' was and the reasons for the police conclusions were given in the report to the Home Office which was considered by the authorities to be final and conclusive.[6]

Bearing in mind that we are still arguing who Jack was 120 years later, it is difficult to accept the Yard's smugness of finality and conclusiveness! Stung by Sims's sneering, the *Pall Mall Gazette* went back to Abberline again and pinned him down on other theories. 'You can state most emphatically,' he told them, 'that Scotland Yard is really no wiser on the subject than it was fifteen years ago. It is simple nonsense to talk of the police having proof that the man is dead. I am, and always have been, in the closest touch with Scotland Yard and it would have been next to impossible for me not to have known about this.'

Abberline produced 'recent documentary evidence' which proved his point, although what that evidence was we do not know.

One by one Abberline batted aside the journalist's probes. Yes, there was a theory that the Whitechapel murderer died in a lunatic asylum, but there was nothing tangible on that. This viewpoint effectively destroys theories involving Aaron Kosminski, Michael Ostrog and William Bury. The journalist mentioned the young medical student [sic] found drowned in the Thames. This of course was Montagu Druitt and he was a lawyer and teacher, not a doctor. 'What does it amount to?' Abberline asked the reporter, 'Simply this. Soon after the last murder [Abberline always believed that this was Mary Kelly's] the body of a young doctor [sic] was found in the Thames but there is absolutely nothing beyond the fact that he was found at that time to incriminate him.'[7]

Researchers like Daniel Farson should have taken note! What about Dr Neill Cream, the reporter asked Abberline. Cream was a psychotic doctor hanged in 1892 for the murder by poison of a prostitute in Lambeth. Addicted to black humour as he was, Cream, according to the hangman James Billington, said, with the hood over his head and the noose around his neck, 'I am Jack the ...' and Billington pulled the lever before he could finish the sentence. Abberline had the answer. 'Neill Cream was not even in this country when the Whitechapel murders took place.' In fact, he was in Joliet State Penitentiary, Illinois, about as watertight an alibi as you can get!

The other professional to cast doubt on Abberline's views on Chapman was Inspector Edmund Reid, who had followed him as local inspector in H Division. He wrote two letters to the *Morning Advertiser* in March and April 1903. From these it is clear that Reid was even wider of the mark than Abberline in terms of Ripper identification. He believed there were nine Ripper victims (Abberline counted six) and that the last was Frances Coles, a prostitute known as Carrotty Nell who was murdered in February 1891. Despite glaring evidence to the contrary, Reid contended that the Ripper showed no medical knowledge whatsoever and that no body parts were removed. He also thought, bizarrely, that the killer used a blunt knife.

So what were the similarities that convinced Abberline that Chapman was the Whitechapel murderer? Allowing for the frenzy of the blitz attacks, there clearly *was* some anatomical awareness for Jack to have removed a kidney, two uteri and a heart. Chapman, as Klosowski, was a trained surgeon. We know he was living in Cable Street, only a few hundred yards from Jack's killing ground, in 1888. He was a 'foreigner' and several eye-witnesses who may have seen the Whitechapel murderer describe him as such. And he was a convicted killer. There, though, the similarities end. Abberline should have read the *Pall Mall Gazette*'s first article more thoroughly. The very first line reads, '... the wretched man now lying under sentence of death for *wife poisoning*' [my italics]. The phenomenon now known as serial murder was almost unknown in 1888. The only phrase in use for someone who killed more than once was 'habitual homicide' and today's definition of a serial killer did not exist. Whoever the Whitechapel murderer was, he was a sexual sadist who carried out blitz attacks with a knife. His victims were random and probably total strangers to him. George Chapman on the other hand was a highly organized murderer, using his medical knowledge to obtain and administer poison. His targets were exclusively his wives.

When challenged over this by the *Gazette* reporter, Abberline stuck to his guns:

> I cannot see why one man should not have done both, provided he had the professional knowledge ... A man who could watch his wives being slowly tortured to death by poison, as he did, is capable of anything ... You see, incentive changes; but the fiendishness is not eradicated. The victims too, you will notice, continue to be women but they are of a different class and obviously call for different methods of dispatch.

Nothing more clearly shows how hopelessly out of their depth were the detectives of 1888 in their efforts to catch Jack. Serial killers find a method of murder which works for them and largely stick to it. Their crimes develop slightly as they grow more confident and inventive, but the social class of victims in the case of sex killers is an irrelevance. Prostitutes are often victims because they are vulnerable, alone on the streets when 'respectable' women are safe in their homes. But Abberline had one other line of thought – the American connection.

The international Press were fascinated by the Ripper case and nowhere more so than in America. In 1888, Richard K. Fox of Franklin Square, New York, published a pamphlet called *The History of the Whitechapel Murders ... with sketches*. It is an extraordinary mix of truth and misconception, but the parts of it that are accurate make it likely that the anonymous author was in London at the time. 'The detectives of Scotland Yard,' he wrote, 'put their heads together, plot, scheme, devise, but all to no purpose.'[8]

The sketches, however, were clearly drawn by someone with no knowledge of British police uniforms, as the body-finding officers are all wearing contemporary American versions that make them look like Mack Sennet's Keystone Kops! 'Misery is written all over the place,' says the author, with reference to Miller's Court, 'the worst kind of London misery – such as those who have lived their lives in America can have no idea of.'

He also chimed in with the general view of the British Press:

The police were, and are, doing nothing of importance ... There is little prospect of anything resulting from the English detectives' efforts. London has resigned itself to wait till the murderer shall betray himself and is already wondering when the next killing will take place.

On 28 September 1888, the last day of the inquest on Annie Chapman, the coroner, Edwin Wynne Baxter, explained during his summing up that he had been approached by the sub-curator of the Pathological Museum[9] who said that some months earlier an American had called on him wanting to obtain wombs for his own medical study at £20 a time. More, he wanted them preserved in glycerine for shipping back to the States. No doubt the public were horrified by this (it was widely reported in the papers over the next few days) but the *Lancet* of 29 September did not find it at all odd as long as the medical research was genuine. What the *Lancet* found unbelievable is that the researcher said he wanted to give away a specimen of a uterus with every book sold – 'the whole tale is almost past belief.'[10]

Wynne Baxter was widely censured for scare-mongering (the man revelled in a certain notoriety) and the information sparked a whole debate on whether the Ripper was an anatomist. The American Press took the story up. A reporter on the *Chicago Tribune* talked to the coroner at Liz Stride's inquest and he denied emphatically that he believed the American researcher to be responsible. The *Tribune* discovered that the man in question was a highly-reputable Philadelphia physician who was willing to pay well for the uteri (although £20 seems to have been Wynne Baxter's 'delusion'). It may be that this 'respectable physician' was Dr Francis Tumblety[11], although he was neither a physician nor reputable.

But in 1903 Abberline's American connection was going in a different direction. 'There is a coincidence also,' he told the *Gazette* reporter, 'in fact that the murders ceased in London when 'Chapman' went to America, while similar murders began to be perpetrated in America after he landed there.'[12]

R. Michael Gordon has tracked down four possible murders which Abberline might have had in mind, all of them occurring, he says, when Chapman was in America. Three are unconvincing. Hannah Robinson was murdered on 2 August 1891. An English-woman from Sunderland, her body was discovered on the edge of the village of Glendale, Long Island, New York. Hannah was a factory worker and nothing about her death is reminiscent of the Ripper. She was manually strangled, with clear finger-mark bruising to her throat and her body had been carefully laid out as if on display. There were no knife wounds at all and no sign of any genital mutilation, very much Jack's signature. While it is true that some serial killers go to great lengths to pose their victims in a grotesque art form, the Ripper's were essentially left where they were killed by a madman in a hurry. Whoever killed Hannah Robinson, it was not the Whitechapel murderer.

Five months later someone murdered Elizabeth Senior. At seventy-three, Elizabeth was older than any of Jack's victims by nearly thirty years. She lived and died in the village of Millburn near Jersey City and, in what was clearly a robbery that went wrong, she was killed in her home in Springfield Avenue on 31 January. The attack on this frail old woman was overkill – there were eleven stab wounds to her breasts and upper torso, her throat had been cut and she had been strangled. Although the police set their sights on a local German-born drunk called August Lyntz, the evidence against him was virtually non-existent and the inquest returned a verdict of 'death at the hands of persons unknown'. The gashes on Mrs Senior's arms reveal defensive wounds. She had time to see her killer burgling her house and to raise her arms instinctively to protect herself. The Ripper, with his blitz attack and savage slash to the throat, worked much faster than that, giving his victims no time to cry out.

The murder of Mary Anderson, which followed on 8 June 1892, is so far removed from Jack's MO as to be laughable. Mary worked as a servant at Maurer's Hotel, Rahway, New Jersey. Her killer shot her in the back with a .32 calibre pistol, cut her throat and dragged her through rough undergrowth to dump her body by the railway line that ran between Perth Amboy and Woodbine Junction. Packages she was carrying were left where she fell and there was no mutilation or any kind of sexual assault.

The only American murder which is actually reminiscent of the Ripper's handiwork is that of Carrie Brown, a prostitute known as Old Shakespeare, on 24 April 1891. She was probably sixty years old and often drunk, although it is possible that she had been a genuine actress earlier in life. She lived and worked in the Tenth Ward, by the East River in New York City. It was the rough equivalent of Whitechapel, with a huge influx of immigrants crowded into a narrow labyrinth of streets. Disease and crime were rampant and whereas the London authorities were blasé about social problems, New York's local government was so riddled with corruption that no improvements were likely to be made in the foreseeable future.

On the last day of her life, Carrie was reeling with drink and looking for business. She found it just before 10.45pm and took her client to Room 31 in the dingy 'flophouse' of the East River Hotel.

At 9.30 the next morning one of the hotel clerks, probably Edward Fitzgerald, found Carrie's body on the bed in No. 31. She was lying on her right side facing the wall with her arm twisted behind her back. She had been disembowelled with a slash that extended from the base of the spine to the front of the abdomen and the letter 'X' had been crudely carved into the skin of her back. The murder weapon – a kitchen knife with a four-inch blade – was found in the room still covered in Old Shakespeare's blood. And there was a great deal of blood – so much in fact that sloppy police officers spread it on their boot soles across to the doorway across the hall. That room belonged to an Algerian called Amir Ben Ali and he was subsequently arrested for the murder.

It did not help that the officer in charge of the Carrie Brown case was Acting Superintendent Thomas Byrnes of the New York Detective Bureau. Byrnes had followed the Ripper case avidly and challenged the killer to come and try his luck in New York as he would catch him in thirty-six hours. In fact his department's track record on homicide was not good and he was forced to resign in 1896 by Police Commissioner Theodore Roosevelt on the grounds of probable corruption. Ben Ali seems to have been a typical 'patsy'. Just as the British police concentrated their efforts on foreigners as likely suspects, so did Byrne's men, and a swarthy Algerian with a poor command of English fitted the bill well. He was pardoned eleven years later.

If Abberline was comparing Carrie Brown's murder in particular he would have been influenced by the banner headlines of the American Press – 'A murder like one of Jack the Ripper's deeds' ... 'Whitechapel's horrors repeated in an East Side Lodging house' ... 'The same horrible act of dismemberment and mutilation which distinguished the Whitechapel atrocities was performed upon this unfortunate hag'. But Abberline should have known better than to take anything the Press said at face value. What he did not see were the post mortem photographs of Carrie Brown, which show a fixation with the anus and that the cuts seem to have been delivered from behind. The very fact that Carrie lay on her side is indicative; all Jack's victims lay on their backs with legs splayed.[13]

There are reputable historians who have spent years researching the Whitechapel murders and there are Ripperologists who have leapt onto passing bandwagons and, in the past at least, written fiction. Abberline, as the most high-profile policeman on the case, has been hijacked by some of these.

The first was novelist, journalist and self-styled criminologist Nigel Morland, who visited Abberline in the 'elegant seaside resort of Bournemouth' in the early 1920s. Abberline had retired from any kind of detective or police work in 1911 and, prosaically enough, Morland found him at work in his garden. The journalist was on a brief period of home leave from his work on a Shanghai newspaper and, although Abberline did not want to talk to him, he eventually relented and said, 'I cannot reveal anything except this – *of course* we knew who he was, one of the highest in the land.' This of course takes us back to the royal connection we examined in the last chapter and was almost certainly never said. There is no corroborative evidence that Morland ever visited Abberline, let alone that the ex-Chief Inspector told him what he did. It not only flies in the face of Abberline's actual work in 1888, when he went after real suspects, all of whom had links to the area and most of whom came from the working class to which Jack's victims belonged, it is also at odds with Abberline's views on Chapman in 1903.

And after Morland, we are in the hands of Donald McCormick. I had the pleasure of meeting this writer and former member of British Intelligence on a totally unrelated writing project. He was charming, witty and with a fund of stories – and that is precisely the problem! His *The Identity of Jack the Ripper* (1959) is laced with errors, fictionalized accounts and invented dialogue that only serves to muddy the factual waters. We are not concerned here with other McCormick myths, merely the one that relates to Abberline and 'Dr Dutton'. Dutton was real enough. He was the second child of George Dutton, manager of the London and Westminster Bank at 130 Whitechapel High Street and was born in 1854, qualifying as a doctor from Durham and Edinburgh universities in 1882. He was an inveterate joiner of philanthropic societies and wrote a number of medical books for the general public. At the time of the Ripper killings he lived at 130 Aldgate High Street, around the corner from Mitre Square, the murder scene of Catherine Eddowes. By the time of his death in 1935, Dutton was known to be fascinated by crime and he kept a diary – the *Chronicles of Crime* – over a sixty-year period. An article in the *Empire News* shortly after his death claimed that he had been chased by a mob back in 1888 because he was carrying a black doctor's bag. The police rescued him and he spent a few days being investigated. If this is so there is no mention of it in the police files. The *Chronicles of Crime* were passed to a Miss Hermione Dudley (who remains untraceable) and were seen by Donald McCormick in 1932. No one has apparently seen them since. Dutton's thesis was the old chestnut about 'Dr Stanley' committing the Whitechapel murders in bitter revenge for the death, from syphilis, of his son. McCormick says in *The Identity* that Abberline and Dutton were friends and that Abberline had suspected Severin Klosowksi at the time of the killings and even interviewed his first mistress, the Polish girl, Lucy Baderski. 'Abberline,' wrote Dutton, 'had long suspected Klosowksi of being the Ripper and discussed the matter with me on many occasions. His original reasons for taking this view were that Klosowksi had actually been seen with one of the Ripper's victims in George Yard [Martha Tabram] on the night of her murder. Then, when he spoke with Lucy Baderski during Klosowski's imprisonment and trial [1903] he was convinced that she, too, suspected her husband ...'

But McCormick/Dutton had another twist in the plot. Lucy Baderski was lying, it seems to inculpate Klosowski rather than have the searchlight of Scotland Yard fall on another alleged suspect, Dr Pedachenko, who just happened to be Klosowski's double!

It is clear by Abberline's response to the *Pall Mall Gazette* reporter in 1903 that it was only reading about George Chapman in the trial reports that he saw a similarity with the Ripper. He had clearly never heard of the man until then. Donald McCormick never let the truth get in the way of a good story. Even if Dutton's *Chronicles of Crime* once existed, all they amount to is the suspicions of an amateur who was living in the killing fields at the time. There is no hard evidence that anything written by Dutton related to the Ripper, or that he knew Abberline. Like much else that Chief Inspector Frederick Abberline did not say, we can consign 'You've got Jack the Ripper at last' to the realms of fiction.

Chapter 10

'Going To Bed with Gentlemen'

Despite the French name, Henry De Pré Labouchère had an impeccable English pedigree. He was educated at Eton and Trinity College Cambridge and served in the Diplomatic Corps between 1854 and 1864. He made his reputation as a fearless campaigner for the truth as a journalist covering the Franco-Prussian War of 1870, writing for the *Daily News* and *The World*. By 1880 he was a Liberal MP for Northampton and editor of the magazine *Truth*. And by that time too he was determined to clean up London – and the rest of the country – in terms of its sordid sexual reputation.

Labouchère particularly had a down on homosexuals and it is a fascinating measure of changing times that today his own homophobia is itself illegal. Whereas prostitution – also one of Labouchère's targets – was widely (if quietly) acknowledged, homosexuality – which Lord Alfred Douglas would famously call 'the love that dare not speak its name' – was completely taboo. Attitudes towards sex between men were strangely ambivalent. Technically a hanging offence in Shakespeare's day, there were only four cases brought in a 120-year period up to 1640, two of which resulted in execution and one of which resulted in a mild reprimand in which the accused did not even bother to turn up to court.

So whereas by Labouchère's time there were prayer meetings and pressure groups like the Society for the Suppression of Vice to combat heterosexual prostitution, there was almost nothing to cope with the homosexual problem. From the 1860s there seems to have been an increase in male prostitution, although figures are notoriously unreliable. The area around Charing Cross and the Strand was one well-known haunt of homosexuals, occasionally called the Maryannes' Mile. The darkness of the shadows under the arches of the Adelphi was perfect for illicit liaisons and the Crown and the

129

Windsor Castle were early examples of 'gay' pubs. In fact, the term 'gay', which usually referred to female prostitutes, was already being hijacked by 1880s homosexuals – although it would be over a century before the term became universal – and they were better known in Labouchère's time as Maryannes, Marjories or Poufs.

The guidebook *More Sprees in London*, circulating widely in the 1870s, recommended 'healthy' female brothels, but warned the public about 'the increase of these monsters in the shapes of men'. Getting into its stride, the magazine went on:

> The wretches are too well paid – principally by rich companions – to care for a few months imprisonment. Why has the pillory been abolished? Can such monsters be held up to too much public degradation and punishment?[1]

Henry Labouchère evidently thought not and busied himself by 1885 in pushing through a Civil Law Amendment Act which would, if not stamp out the 'bestiality' entirely, at least give homosexuals pause. Labouchère's original idea had been to bring in sentences of seven years hard labour to life imprisonment and the definition of the offence was 'gross indecency'. In fact this was never clearly defined, perhaps because parliament was too embarrassed to go into detail. Famously, too, 'Labouchère's Amendment' was to include female homosexuality, but since the queen thought a Lesbian was an inhabitant of the Greek island of Lesbos, she vetoed that proposal – the last time in constitutional history that a reigning monarch has done so. So, in a blatant example of sexism an unusual way round, for seventy-two years there was a law which women were above. Because 'Labouchère's Amendment' spoke of acts in private as well as public, the whole thing came to be known as the 'blackmailers' charter' and was not repealed until 1967.

On 4 July 1889 Post Office Constable 718 Luke Hankes was called in to investigate a series of thefts from the General Post Office headquarters at St Martin's-le-Grand. The suspect was fifteen-year-old Charles Swinscow, who had been found with eighteen shillings in cash in his pockets, far above what a post-boy was likely to earn in several months. Swinscow's statement was that he had earned the money (only fourteen shillings, he claimed) from a man named Hammond who lived at 19 Cleveland Street opposite the sprawling

Middlesex Hospital. When asked what the money paid by Hammond was for, Swinscow told Constable Hankes it was 'for going to bed with gentlemen at his house'.

What came to be known as the Cleveland Street scandal emerged by accident, as the result of a routine check on a postal worker who was not supposed to be carrying money at all. In the days before widespread High Street banking, boys like Swinscow took cheques and postal orders to businesses all over major cities and the General Post Office had a formidable reputation for efficiency and honesty which was the envy of the world. In fact, Swinscow may have been delighted to explain the origin of the cash, because it cleared him of any suspicion of theft. In the event once he started talking it was difficult to shut him up.

Swinscow's story was that he had been seduced by an older boy, Henry Newlove, by now a junior clerk. They had gone into the toilets in the Post Office building and 'behaved indecently together'. It was only a short step from this to Newlove's suggestion that Swinscow could earn four shillings a time for doing the same thing with gentlemen. Accordingly, he took the initiate to 19 Cleveland Street and met the proprietor, Mr Hammond. Hammond in turn introduced Swinscow to 'another gentleman' and the pair of them went into a bedroom.

> We both undressed and both being quite naked got into the bed. He put his penis between my legs and an emission took place. I was with him about ½ an hour and then we got up. He gave me a sovereign which I gave to Mr Hammond who gave me 4 shillings.[2]

Swinscow had gone back once more, this time to entertain a different gentleman.

We can imagine the wording here – 'penis', 'emission' is Hankes's attempt to follow the letter of the law. A fifteen-year-old postal boy would have his own slang which would be inadmissible in court. At fifteen, Swinscow was not a minor, but the evidence, if true, made it clear that Hammond was running a male brothel at No. 19.

And Swinscow was still talking. He named other boys who were his colleagues – George Wright and Charles Thickbroom, although the story kept coming back to Newlove and Hammond. All the boys were suspended, but the shock of Swinscow's confession sent waves eddying all the way to Whitehall. 'Surely,' ranted Henry Labouchère in the Commons once the scandal had reached the Press, 'it [No. 19] must have been known to the police and if it was not known to them it ought to have been.'[3]

So carried away was he with his crusading rhetoric that he came out with a prize piece of nonsense – 'In no other cities in the world are such abominations openly carried on.'

The chain of command in the Post Office ended with the Postmaster-General, Henry Raikes MP, who in turn contacted Commissioner James Monro at Scotland Yard. This efficient and popular Scotsman had recently been at loggerheads with Sir Charles Warren when he had been Warren's subordinate in charge of crime. As authoritarian as the general, Monro had got used to running things his own way and reporting directly to the Home Secretary, Henry Matthews, rather than going through Warren himself. With Warren's resignation in November 1888 however, Monro was promoted to what turned out to be the briefest tenure of Commissioner in the history of the job (he resigned in 1890). Monro sent for Abberline.

Several writers on the Cleveland Street scandal have pointed to Abberline's involvement as very telling, because he was still up to his neck in the Whitechapel murders and so Cleveland Street's priority spoke volumes for the government's need to have the whole thing handled quickly, quietly and by a man with a reputation for tact and discretion. In fact, since November 1888 the Ripper case had been scaled down and, despite the attack on prostitute Annie Farmer on 20 November and the murder of Rose Mylett one month later, the Whitechapel scare appeared to be a thing of the past. The murder of Alice McKenzie, which may have been Jack's handiwork, did not occur until 17 July 1889, by which time Abberline was on the Cleveland Street case. The last we hear of him in the context of Whitechapel is March 1889.

As always, Abberline moved fast. On Saturday 6 July he set up a special sitting of the Marlborough Street magistrates court at which Swinscow, Wright and Thickbroom appeared. The result of this was that Abberline now had arrest warrants for Newlove and Hammond 'that they did unlawfully, wickedly and corruptly conspire, combine and confederate and agree to incite and procure George Alma Wright and divers other persons to commit the abominable crime of buggery' which, apparently, was 'not to be named among Christians' and was somehow 'against the peace'.[4]

Abberline and his team descended on No. 19 to find it deserted, the first blow in what was to be a series of bitter disappointments in this case. It is likely that Newlove, who was arrested by Constable Hankes at his mother's house in Bayham Street, Camden, the next day, had tipped Hammond off and the brothel-keeper had caught a steam packet from Gravesend to France.

Furious that he had been left in the lurch, Newlove gave other names to Hankes, including 'men in high position', Lord Arthur Somerset, the Earl of Euston and Colonel Jervois. He gave the same names to Abberline on Monday 8 July and the inspector had the house in Cleveland Street watched from then on. Of the plain-clothes team that must have been involved in this, Constable Sladden of D Division, Tottenham Court Road, seems to have been the most observant. Several of the visitors were soldiers, including a corporal in the Life Guards, and for Sladden to be sure of this, the man had to be wearing his undress scarlet uniform or he could not have been sure of his regiment. His log for 10 July still survives, noting the arrival of two women, one of whom was Hammond's sister-in-law at 2.05pm. Two and a half hours later, Lord Arthur Somerset arrived in a hansom cab and waited until 5.10 when a corporal of the 2nd Battalion[5] Life Guards met him, 'apparently by appointment'. They shook hands, which is something an officer and an enlisted man *never* did. While these comings and goings were noted, Abberline's team were carrying out a lightning 'Who's Who' of the great and not so good of London society. Lord Arthur Somerset, known to his circle as 'Podge', was a crony of the Prince of Wales with the title of Superintendent of the Stables and Extra Equerry. His father was the Duke of Beaufort with a huge estate at Badminton in Gloucestershire and was known behind the closed doors of the aristocracy for his penchant for under-age girls. Clearly, Arthur and his younger brother, Henry, swung in another direction entirely. For convention's sake, Henry had married but his wife left him after she discovered her husband's predilection for footmen in his service.

The Earl of Euston was Henry Fitzroy, son of the Duke of Grafton, who had married Kate Walsh in St Michael's Church, Worcester, in 1871. Like many wealthy men of his day, Euston had a penchant for illicit sex and claimed, as we shall see, that he went to No. 19 by mistake, thinking it to be an establishment for *poses plastiques*, a sort of immobile strip club which pandered largely to older men. Recent research, almost certainly unknown to Abberline, suggests that Euston was bisexual and was being blackmailed, thanks to Henry Labouchère's Amendment, by Robert Cliburn, who specialised in fleecing older men with a reputation to uphold.

Henry Jervois is the most obscure of all the minor celebrities to visit Hammond's establishment. There is a colonel of artillery in the Army Lists with the same surname, but it cannot be the same man because he was posted abroad at the time. Perhaps 'Colonel Jervois' was an alias.

By 19 July Abberline had submitted his report to Monro, who handed it over to the Treasury Solicitor, Sir Augustus Stephenson. With names like these in the frame, Stephenson got cold feet and passed it back to the police, who had no alternative but to approach Henry Matthews, who duly passed the case on to the Director of Public Prosecutions (who happened to be Augustus Stephenson, so the wheel came full circle). In the meantime, Abberline pressed for extradition papers for Hammond. Everybody, from Matthews down, must have been surprised at the intervention at that stage of the Prime Minister, Lord Salisbury. Acting in his role as Foreign Secretary, Salisbury sent a reply to Matthews on 24 July:

> I am now directed to inform you ... that his lordship [Salisbury] does not consider this to be a case in which any official application could justifiably be made to the French Government ...

We know from Abberline's earlier cases, especially the Fenian Dynamitards, how difficult the French could be in complying with British requests; but here was the head of Her Majesty's government not even trying. It stank to Heaven. On 25 July the DPP took up the case formally (Hammond by now had been gone for three weeks), intending to bring a case against Newlove, Hammond and an unsavoury character called George Veck, a former telegraphist with the Post Office who had been dismissed for interfering with messenger boys at Gravesend. Now calling himself 'The Reverend' he appears to have been in business with Hammond and had promised Newlove's mother that he had sufficient cash to look after the boy.

Abberline put a discreet watch on Lord Arthur Somerset, both on his London home and the Knightsbridge cavalry barracks where he usually spent his days. By 10 August, the DPP had decided to proceed against Somerset under Section XI of the Criminal Law Amendment Act (Labouchère's) and to bring Veck and Hammond to trial too. Critics of Abberline and the establishment complain that the whole process dragged on interminably, but the machinery of the law is always slow and by the standards of the 1880s, the process seems to have been carried out efficiently and quickly. Now Lord Salisbury stepped in again, anxious to keep Somerset's name out of it. The man was too close to the Prince of Wales and none of this must reach the Press.

Abberline went in person to Paris. We know that his French was halting at best and unsurprisingly he got short change from the Parisian police. The Paris Prefecture was a notoriously corrupt institution, rather like Thomas Byrnes's New York force, and the long tradition of hostility between Britain and France meant that cases like Hammond's would remain very low on the list of French priorities.

And the government's feet grew even colder. On 17 August, Sir Richard Webster, the Attorney General, wrote to Augustus Stephenson on the discrepancies between the accounts of Swinscow, Thickbroom and Constable Sladden and now doubted whether they were describing Lord Arthur Somerset at all. He was happy to proceed against Veck, however, and Abberline's men crashed through the door of the man's lodgings in Howland Street, a stone's throw from Hammond's brothel, early in the morning on 19 August. In bed was seventeen-year-old George Barber, calling himself Veck's 'private secretary'. Veck himself was picked up at Waterloo station later that day. In his pocket were papers referring to a 'Mr Brown' and Algernon Allies of Gregory Street, Sudbury, on the Suffolk/Essex border.

Allies was a perfect witness for Abberline. He had been picked up by Somerset when he worked as a page boy in the Marlborough Club. When he lost his job there for theft, Somerset took him in at his London address at 19 Hill Street. It was a letter of introduction from Somerset that got Allies a permanent post with Hammond and the noble lord, calling himself 'Mr Brown', sent Allies money and love letters, none of which the lad still had. He had been tipped off, probably by Veck, and had burned all the correspondence. Now, under Abberline's protection, Allies was taken to a 'safe house' above the Rose, a coffee house in Houndsditch, and was carefully guarded.

Once again the authorities hedged. 'Mr Brown' or 'LAS' as he is referred to coyly in official papers, still might not be Lord Arthur Somerset or, if it was, he could have been the totally innocent victim of a conspiracy by the messenger boys. Augustus Stephenson even went so far as to try to whitewash the whole case:

> I am quite aware that although it is a legal offence to keep a bawdy house – it is not a legal offence to keep or frequent a house for the accommodation of sodomites.

He was splitting hairs here. Labouchère's Amendment made it clear that sex between men was illegal even if in private. That meant that all visitors could be charged, from Swinscow to Somerset, and Hammond could be charged with procuring. Stephenson was behaving as if No. 19 itself was the subject of possible police charges!

It may be that Abberline was only too aware that the big fish might yet slip through the net and he did his best to find as much evidence as he could. He found John Saul of 150 Old Compton Street, Soho, and he had an interesting story to tell. Saul seems to have been a copper's nark, that phrase that 'Dolly' Williamson so hated, but whether he was an informant just for Abberline is unknown. Saul was ready to admit that both he and Hammond 'earned our livelihood as sodomites'[6] and the pair shared lodgings late in 1879. Hammond was continually on the move, had married a (female) French prostitute and was in the habit of procuring Post Office boys to attract rich clients. Saul named names exactly as the others had done and included 'the young Duke of Grafton, I mean the brother of the present Duke [in other words, the Earl of Euston].'

Saul made two statements to Abberline and even produced 'Maryannes' calling cards belonging to two men who accompanied Euston to Hammond's establishment. Euston, who would later claim that he was just visiting to see some *poses plastiques*, 'likes to play with you,' Saul told Abberline, 'and then "spend" on your belly.'[7] Abberline's problem – and one major reason why Saul's statements never appeared in court – is that the man was flaky. He was in his late thirties, past his best and bitter. The notes he had compiled, which found a permanent existence in an underground book called *Cities of the Plain*, were so bizarre that some of the information at least is likely to be fiction. No court in 1889 would accept them. But, just in case, by the end of August Lord Arthur Somerset applied for four months leave from the army and sailed for Europe.

He did so just before Cleveland Street hit the fan. The committal proceedings against Veck and Newlove had produced no actual names and the Press became suspicious. William Stead's crusading *Pall Mall Gazette* cut to the chase at once:

> The wretched agents [Veck and Newlove] are run in and sent to penal servitude; the lords and gentlemen who employ them swagger at large and are even welcomed as valuable allies of the Administration of the day.[8]

The Man of the World went further, placing two seemingly unconnected articles side by side. 'Lord Arthur Somerset has left England,' said one; 'A gross scandal ... has been discovered by the police ...' said the other, leaving the readership in no doubt that something unsavoury was afoot.

Augustus Stephenson was still vainly trying to move against Somerset when the rumour reached him that Newlove's solicitor, the decidedly dodgy Arthur Newton, was preparing to implicate 'a very distinguished person ... (P.A.V.).'[9]

Prince Albert Victor hovers like a ghost around Abberline at this point in his career. We have seen already the nonsense concocted by Joseph Sickert and Stephen Knight involving the 'highest in the land' and here he is again. The implication was plain. 'Podge' was a close friend of the Prince of Wales, Eddie's father, and what was more 'natural' than that the lad should be taken on sexual sprees involving both sexes as part of the future king's education? Eddie wasn't very bright and, because of the deafness possibly inherited from his mother, found learning very difficult. Examinations were simplified for him and he left Cambridge with a very unlikely honorary degree of Doctor of Law. He rose to the rank of major, but only in his father's regiment, the 10th Hussars, where he became known, somewhat disparagingly, as 'the pet of the 10th', as though he was some sort of regimental mascot! But he was not Jack the Ripper or the 'reason' for Jack the Ripper, and there is no evidence at all that he ever went near 19 Cleveland Street or any other brothel, male or female.

In the ensuing trial of Newlove and Veck (and Hammond, *in absentia*) seventeen counts stood against them. In the event a deal was struck – Newlove pleaded guilty to thirteen counts, Veck to two. Newlove got four months gaol; Veck, nine. The whole proceedings were over in an hour and there was no court reporter present. Could there be a surer example of the powers that be sweeping things under the carpet?

On 25 September, however, all that promised to change. Algernon Allies received a visitor at the safe house and Abberline immediately took Allies's statement in connection with it. A tall, fair gentleman in his mid-twenties offered the rent boy £15, clothes and a passage to America to begin a new life. Allies arranged to meet the man to push things forward and Abberline and Hankes were waiting. The rendezvous was outside the A1 pub in Tottenham Court Road and the policemen recognized Augustus de Gallo, a private detective who worked for the solicitor Arthur Newton. When the young man turned up he gave Abberline his name and business, but nothing more. He was Frederick Taylerson, Newton's clerk.

This was a clear case of attempting to bribe a witness and Abberline applied for an arrest warrant. Once again the powers that be above Monro prevaricated and Arthur Newton (who would later be struck off and imprisoned) launched into ludicrous invective against Abberline. The Inspector had kept Allies in the Rose 'in a state of duress'. He had been threatened and told not to leave the premises. His letters to his family were dictated. Allies's father wanted the boy to leave the country; Allies wanted to leave the country. Only the 'threats made by the police' made this impossible. When Taylerson had met up with Allies (odd in itself in that Newton had said he was unable to leave the Rose) Abberline and Hankes 'had the audacity to detain [Taylerson].'[10]

But it was what happened the next day that blew the matter sky high. The *North London Press*, a low-circulation tabloid edited by Ernest Parke, ran a story on Cleveland Street. The trial of Newlove and Veck had been held, asserted the paper, virtually in secret; Hammond had been allowed to escape (he was believed to be in Belgium by this time); the sentences were shockingly lenient; and various members of the aristocracy were involved. *Reynold's Newspaper*, with an almost national circulation, took up the tale the next day. The fact that Parke was prepared to name names implied that he had seen witness statements, but exactly who leaked them remains unclear. It may have been a deliberate ploy to kick-start officials in the corridors of power. And of course the leak could have come from Abberline.

The inspector issued subpoenas on Allies and the other lads to appear as witnesses against Hammond at the Old Bailey on 21 October. In the meantime, John Phillips of the Post Office Confidential Inquiry Bureau trailed Hammond all over France while the brothel-keeper wrote desperate begging letters for urgent cash to anyone he could think of. Abberline had joined Phillips, as we have seen, but he was replaced by Inspector Lowe, also of the Yard, as Abberline was too crucial to be left languishing in the fleshpots of Paris. It was Phillips who followed Hammond to Halenzy in Belgium and, by the end of the month, Lowe was in turn replaced by Inspector Greenham.

But Newton and others made sure that Hammond made good his escape. On 5 October, Hammond, his wife Caroline, Frederick Taylerson and Hammond's amanuensis Bertie Ames sailed for New York from Antwerp on the SS *Pennland*. They ended up in Seattle, Washington Territory, which would become a state in the following month.

By early October, things seemed to have simmered down to the extent that Lord Arthur Somerset felt safe to return to England, if only for his grandmother's funeral. Monro, no doubt urged by

Abberline, pushed for an arrest warrant and Constable Hankes was given the job of following Somerset, hovering on the edge of the family's funeral cortège at Badminton. Still the authorities dithered. The Lord Chancellor, Lord Halsbury, was the country's senior law lord and a crawler. He pointed out in writing to the DPP's office that Somerset's crime (if guilty) was only a misdemeanour and probably wouldn't work anyway. He was also concerned about the probity of witnesses like Saul, Newlove and Veck – 'People do not do these things in the presence of persons of respectability as a rule.'[11]

Monro wrote to Hamilton Cuffe, Stephenson's number two at the DPP, furious at still further delay. He also threatened to put the obnoxious Mr Newton in his place: 'If he tries any more of his objectionable letters, I suggest your referring him to the Police. We shall deal with him.'[12]

The fact that Newton was threatening to drag Prince Albert Victor's name through the mud meant that Monro's heroics had to be muted and he was leaned on by two very distinguished courtiers, Sir Dighton Probyn VC and Sir Francis Knollys, private secretary to the Prince of Wales. Monro would not be leaned on, but clearly those above him would and Somerset was again allowed to leave the country on 18 October. The eventual issue of a warrant for his arrest, on charges of gross indecency with Allies and Thickbroom at Cleveland Street was largely, as it turned out, a waste of time. At least Somerset had the integrity to resign his commission.

By 16 November Ernest Parke had had enough. Under a headline 'the Distinguished Criminals who have Escaped', he named the Earl of Euston and Lord Arthur Somerset. For good measure, but without actual names, he referred to 'two or three members of parliament, one of them being a popular Liberal' as frequenters of Hammond's now instantly notorious No. 19. An incandescent Lord Euston had Parke charged with criminal libel and two armed camps were formed – the aristocracy, effectively spearheaded by the Prince of Wales, not to mention various government hangers-on and the bulk of the Conservative well-to-do, against the freedom of the Press brigade and the entire working class.

The foreign Press got hold of all this, in particular the American papers. They had no hesitation in throwing Prince Albert Victor's name into the mix, one of them leading with a savage anti-royal denunciation far exceeding anything Henry Labouchère had to say:

> The inbred crowd of royal stock of all Europe is becoming sadly deteriorated both bodily and mentally ... whether England will ever have a king after the Prince of Wales is a matter of speculation.

Dogged as ever, Abberline ordered Constable Sladden, who had formed a paternal bond with Thickbroom and the others, to take the boys to St James's clubs and other haunts of gentlemen to point out any visitors to No. 19. The boys had been dismissed by the Post Office and were hoping that someone could help them. That someone turned out to be Arthur Newton, who was prepared to fund their emigration to Australia. Unfortunately for him, the boys told Abberline and a warrant was duly issued against him on a charge of conspiring to 'obstruct, pervert and defeat the due course of the law'. Allies was moved from the Rose and not even his family knew where he was.

Ernest Parke's trial began at the Old Bailey on 15 January 1890. Sir Henry 'Hanging' Hawkins presided as judge and Sir Charles Russell QC appeared for Euston. Frank Lockwood defended Parke. It was now that Euston's counsel trotted out the story of his client being inveigled to visit No. 19 to see *poses plastiques* and acknowledged that it did him no credit. The law at the time said that ladies could pose naked as long as they did not move – all this was a far cry from the sodomy hinted at by Parke. Above all, Euston, realizing that he had been conned, had not returned and was certainly not a frequent visitor to the place.

At this point, the whole thing descended into farce. Various witnesses who said they had seen Euston visit Cleveland Street on several occasions turned out to be 'stage Irishmen' – 'My sight is very queer since' ... 'He [Euston] was like an old policeman who had twenty years on the stones' ... 'His trousers were so loose that one leg of them would have made me a pair.' Most damning was the fact that one of them said they had been promised money from the detective agency that had found him and another that Euston was about his own height (five feet eight inches) whereas actually the noble lord was six feet four inches.

John Saul was far more credible – or should have been were it not for the prudery and homophobia of the court. He had actually had sex with Euston – although *The Times* reporter could not print that – but was easily demolished by Russell because of his shady past. Russell even managed to discredit the Metropolitan Police by inferring that they habitually turned blind eyes to homosexuality in the metropolis. We can imagine the jury listening in horror to references to men called Viola and Queen Anne. In the dock, Euston was impeccable – assured, unruffled, every inch aware of the unreliable nature of the witnesses against him without Hammond's presence.

And if Abberline hoped for an impartial summing-up from 'Hanging' Hawkins, he was to be disappointed. Hawkins hoped that the police were not kind to Saul because the judge had never seen 'a more melancholy spectacle, a more loathsome object' than the male prostitute. Hawkins then turned on Abberline – if he had taken Saul's statement all those months before, why hadn't Euston been arrested and charged? What was Abberline doing unless he knew Saul's story to be false? He spoke for two and a half hours and the jury returned the verdict after a further forty-five minutes – 'Guilty of libel without justification'. Hawkins sent Parke down for twelve months without hard labour and such was the prudery of the establishment in 1890 that today the online proceedings of the Old Bailey case merely say 'the details of this case were unfit for publication'.

Again, there were armed camps, pro- and anti-Parke. *The Labour Elector* was particularly vitriolic: 'If Lord Euston had gone to [Parke's office] and there and then physically twisted the little wretch's neck nobody would have blamed him.'

The Elector wanted penal servitude for life in Parke's case. As it was, the *North London Press* died with its editor's incarceration, appearing for the last time at the end of January. Frank Harris, on the other hand, found the sentence far too harsh and claimed that Hawkins had handed it out to secure his own advancement. Since he later became Baron Brompton it may be that Harris had a point.

The Cleveland Street scandal threatened to rock the upper echelons of society but failed to do so as those echelons closed ranks and lied their way out of trouble. As a postscript, the authors of one of the best accounts of the subject[13] say this of Abberline:

Inspector Frederick Abberline also appears to have suffered some loss of status. The whimpering end of the Cleveland Street Affair [the conviction and imprisonment of Arthur Newton] was for him the postscript of two years of frustration. His record as one of Scotland Yard's ace detectives was by April 1890 overlaid by the image of the detective who failed to solve the Jack the Ripper murders and who had let Lord Arthur Somerset slip out of his grasp while in possession of immaculate evidence on the Cleveland Street case. Abberline's reputation never fully recovered.

This is not strictly true. Abberline certainly failed to catch Jack, but in that context he stood shoulder to shoulder with everybody else in the Metropolitan and City forces and the reasons for it are identified elsewhere. In the case of Cleveland Street, his evidence against Somerset was never 'immaculate' and he was too far down the chain of command to make any move without his superiors' say so. Had he done so, Somerset would have walked on a technicality. It is evident from the facts that the police, from the resourceful, keenly observant Hankes and Sladden up to Commissioner Monro himself, worked with speed, diligence and efficiency to carry out their jobs and observe the letter of the law, however much we might disagree with that law today. The problem was what lay above Monro – the brick wall of the old school tie brigade who closed ranks to protect their own. Even with the promotion to chief inspector given to him in 1890, Abberline could not crack that.[14]

Chapter 11

'We Never Sleep!'

Because the Ripper case and the Cleveland Street scandal were – and remain – such lurid flashpoints of interest, retiring to the humdrum routine of London's crime scene seems anti-climactic. It was much more satisfying aesthetically for Frederick Abberline to die romantically, as Johnny Depp did in *From Hell*. In fact, in terms of years, he had nearly half his life still to live and he worked in various capacities as a law enforcer for another fifteen.

We do not know where Abberline and his wife were living after his transfer to Scotland Yard in 1887, but perhaps his promotion to chief inspector just before Christmas 1890 warranted a further move anyway. The census of 1891, taken six months later, gives their address as 41 Mayflower Road, Clapham; the house is still there. An Anne Polisford, originally of Tiverton, Devon, is also listed there. She was Abberline's age (forty-eight), but it is not clear whether she was a landlady or housekeeper.

In March of that year, Abberline oversaw a case of obtaining money by false pretences involving Joseph and Annie Roodhouse. The *Daily Telegraph* reported under a banner headline 'Alleged Traffic in Infants' and touched on the baby-farming spate of crimes which culminated in the notorious Amelia Dyer being hanged in 1896 for the killing of several children in Reading. The Roodhouses were in the business for the same reason – financial gain – but drew the line at murder. They had advertised in newspapers posing as a childless couple longing for a baby and Caroline Colbatch, a servant, replied. An unmarried servant with a noisy, demanding child was not likely to keep her post long and the Roodhouses' advertisement may have come as manna from heaven to the girl. Using a fictitious address in Birmingham, Annie Roodhouse signed the adoption papers and duly gurgled over the child, but Joseph was less impressed by the baby and he was passed to a Mrs Heeling of Ellis Street, Tidal Basin, whose dock labourer husband seemed perfectly happy to believe the baby was his! Mr Horace Avery, prosecuting at Bow Street police court, had never come across this level of deception before and was clearly horrified by it. Abberline's arrest of the Roodhouses uncovered scams involving the use of poste restantes and false occupations in which the couple received anything between £3 and £25 for the 'adoption' to take place. Abberline found the transaction book which contained the names and addresses of over 100 women who had given their babies away in a fraught mixture of hope and desperation.

The same hope and desperation of course can be seen in those wishing to adopt – who also paid the Roodhouses handsomely. Mrs Heeling was one of those who had replied to the advertisement, 'would any lady adopt infant from birth for love only?' She signed a paper in Annie Roodhouse's presence to be kind to the child and assured the court that a docker earned good money and would bring up the boy according to strict principles. There was a great deal of laughter in court at this.

Despite the element of farce, the baby-farming aspects were horrendous. In many cases there was no actual record of where the children ended up. One child who was traced was 'ravenously hungry, filthy and suffering from bronchitis or suppressed measles.'[1]

When the *Sunday World* got hold of the story, the New Journalism of the day kicked in. 'It is a case which we might expect to find only in the notebook of one of those gentlemen who write "detective stories" for light periodicals.' They were no doubt thinking of Arthur Conan Doyle, whose Sherlock Holmes tales were now appearing in *The Strand* magazine. The '*World* man' sent to interview Abberline quoted him as saying he had never come across a case like this before and saying 'Rather a pretty name is Roodhouse.' Such ruminations sound far more like the *World* man's attempt at colour than anything Abberline might have said. But the *Sunday World* was sniping in all directions – 'we all know that in one of the most delightful of the Gilbert and Sullivan operas, "HMS Pinafore" there is a little lady who confesses that she had practised baby farming, "Dear Little Buttercup"; baby farming was, no doubt, very harmless.'[2]

Sir Thomas Chambers, the Recorder (judge) who handled the case had likewise never come across this sort of crime before and he delayed sentence until he had a chance to confer with his colleagues. In the end, Joseph Roodhouse got eighteen months hard labour and his wife twelve. Abberline must have been spitting; he believed that as many as ten children had died of neglect as a result of the Roodhouses' transactions.

The last case that Abberline handled at the Yard was a complicated deception by Frederick Peach and Walter Selwyn (aka Melville). It involved large sums of money and even though the use of the name Retlaw Newles by Selwyn seems puerile to us now, it was a clever scam at the time. When he appeared in the witness box at the Old Bailey, Abberline said, 'I was for many years in the police force. I have lately retired, in my thirtieth year of service. I was then chief inspector.' He was believed to have saved British investors thousands of pounds by nailing these two.

The sudden departure of the chief inspector has been seized on by conspiracy theorists of every hue. He knew the 'truth' about the Ripper murders. He had Prince Albert Victor in the frame for Cleveland Street. And he either resigned on a point of principle over one or both of them or he was paid hush money to move on, somewhere where his investigative skills would not penetrate the murky gloom of the corridors of power.

Unfortunately for such theorists, the real reason for his going is all about timing and money and it is rather prosaic. Police pensions had been low – and a source of bitterness – since 1849. They were discretionary and even officers injured in the line of duty did not necessarily qualify. The two police strikes of 1872 and 1890 had been largely over this grievance, but the Police Act of 1890 tackled the problem at last. All officers who had served for twenty-five years (Abberline had served twenty-seven by then) were to receive half pay as pension. As he was still only forty-nine in 1892 he obviously judged the time was right to go.

On 4 January the *Pall Mall Gazette* trumpeted his farewell:

Mr Abberline's retirement … will be felt as a great loss at Scotland Yard where he has always been regarded as one of the most efficient officers of the Department and was constantly entrusted with cases requiring courage, skill and discretion. He has consequently had opportunities of distinction in connection with some of the most important investigations with which Scotland yard has had to deal.[3]

On 8 June of the same year, when he had been absent from the Yard for nearly six months, a presentation was held in his honour by his colleagues from the force. It was held at the Three Nuns Hotel, Aldgate, an impressive Gothic-looking building between St Botolph's church and Aldgate Underground Station and opposite the Minories. Various speeches were given along with numerous toasts. Abberline was congratulated and thanked on behalf of the people of the East End and the turnout was huge. Superintendent Arnold was there from H Division and Superintendent Jones from G. John Shore represented the senior end of the Yard itself and there were fourteen detective inspectors, one of whom, Frank Froest, was already in the Special Irish Branch and would become a super-intendent himself by 1906. The great and good of Whitechapel were represented by Isaac David and one of the guests was a J. McCarthy, who *may* have been the John McCarthy who was Mary Kelly's land-lord and owned property all over the Abyss. They gave Abberline a silver salver inscribed with the words 'in the honourable service of that department of our system which had for its object the detection of crime'. He was also given a 'valuable tea and coffee set, weighing in aggregate 140 ounces of silver'.[4]

The chairman said that John Bull [the average Englishman] was a great grumbler and that one of the things he grumbled about was the police force, which, it was alleged, was never as good as that of France, Germany, Russia or the United States. But what they did in these police forces 'would not be tolerated for a moment in free England'. The cheers were deafening.

Abberline replied that he was delighted to see so many old friends there, both in the force and out of it. Whitechapel, he knew, was at last receiving the kind of help and funding which it so desperately needed and the Met, now numbering over 15,000 men, had served and continued to serve London with courage and distinction.

The warmest praise of all came from Thomas Arnold. Losing Abberline, he said, was like losing his right hand and he would find it very difficult to replace the man. He mentioned the Ripper:

when I was in trouble during the continuance of the White-chapel crimes, Mr Abberline came down to the East End and gave the whole of his time with the object of bringing these crimes to light. Unfortunately, however, the circumstances were such that success was impossible but it was no fault of Mr Abberline's that they did not succeed.[5]

But Abberline's resignation from the Met was not quite a leap in the dark. In the handwritten notes accompanying his cuttings book he said:

after I left the Metropolitan Police Service on a pension I was engaged from time to time in making private enquiries for various business houses etc. but I always declined domestic matters such as divorce as they were repugnant to my feelings.[6]

The exact nature of the Victorian private detective's work is shadowy and vague, not helped in the least by the fact that the 1880–90s saw the emergence of a fictional one who so caught the public's imagination that he is still 'the world's greatest detective' – Sherlock Holmes. Abberline's reluctance to take on domestic cases meant that he was turning down money, but that element of the job has always conjured up a picture of seedy men in mackintoshes working out of rundown offices. So powerful is this image that, hard on the heels of Sherlock Holmes, came a whole series of amateur sleuths from aristocrats like Dorothy L. Sayers's Lord Peter Wimsey to Raymond Chandler's 'hard-boiled' Philip Marlowe. The dubious nature of private investigators is made clear by other men who joined their ranks. John Meiklejohn, disgraced, dismissed from the Met and imprisoned after the Trial of the Detectives in 1877 is an example. So is the pairing of Batchelor and Grand who worked in the Ripper case. Charles Grand (or more usually Le Grand) was probably born Christian Briscony in about 1853 and was known to have used at least six aliases. He had a criminal record and was possibly the son of a Danish diplomat before disgracing his family by serving eight years in prison for theft. His paranoia showed through in 1897 when he wrote to the Commissioner, Charles Warren, threatening to burn down buildings and alleging brutality from a police constable.

Exactly when he went into the private enquiry business with J.H. Batchelor is unknown, but they were certainly operating out of offices in the Strand by the time of the Ripper murders. Batchelor may have been the James Batchelor who ran the Lion pub at 309 The Strand. Both of them were probably con men and they put pressure on the fruiterer Matthew Packer at the time of Elizabeth Stride's murder yards from the grocer's shop. They took Packer to see the corpse in the mortuary at St George's-in-the-East and quite possibly invented the whole grape story which has bedevilled the Ripper enquiry ever since (at least in fiction). The pair worked in this period for the *Evening News* and *Daily Telegraph* and coordinated the night operations of the Whitechapel Vigilance Committee.

The following year Grand was in trouble again and went down for two years for sending threatening letters to Malcolm Morris, a Harley street surgeon. In 1891, now called Charles Grant, he was again sending vicious letters to various ladies demanding money with menaces. Even Batchelor seems to have had enough by this time and gave evidence against him in court.

Clearly, Abberline's position was very different. As an ex-Scotland Yard officer, he knew everybody on both sides of the criminal fence and his prestige was immense, both in terms of the cases he undertook and the results he got. He no longer had the resources of the Met, but he had the experience that his long service had given him. 'Calling in the Yard' for serious crimes like murder had been going on certainly since the 1860s, when Jonathan Whicher was sent to investigate the murder at Road, so Abberline himself had also travelled across the country and abroad in his routine enquiries. Sadly, his actual work as a private investigator is almost a closed book. He wrote twenty-eight pages in long-hand which he called his *Reminiscences* and they were probably part of a much longer work that he either never produced or that has been lost.[7] Most of it deals with a single case which might have appropriately been called 'the lady vanishes'.

Abberline was no Arthur Conan Doyle and yet the tale of the disappearing woman is strangely gripping. Abberline's problem as writer – assuming he intended this for publication one day – is that all his instincts and the caveats from the Yard hierarchy told him not to do it. He also had the laws of libel to contend with and that leaves us with an infuriatingly vague story with no real names or locations to add authenticity. What is almost certainly a true story reads like rather bad fiction. Inspector Maurice Moser, whose *Stories from Scotland Yard* was published while Abberline was still a serving officer, was forced into the same trap, although he at least had a ghost writer, Charles F. Rideal. Ex-Chief Inspector Cavanagh of M Division went into print in 1893 after thirty-seven years with the Met and he cannot name names either. Even Chief Inspector John Littlechild of the Special Irish Branch, whose *Reminiscences* were written in 1894 (more or less at the same time as Abberline's) had to invent letters for names or leave blanks in the text. The sub-heading of Abberline's missing persons case is dreadful – 'The mysterious disappearance of a lady supposed decoyed away from home for robbery and perhaps murdered and her strange adventure.'

We have no idea whether Abberline took offices or had staff. He may simply have worked from home, probably in Clapham and alone. This particular case came directly from the Commissioner, who, although Abberline does not name him, was Sir Edward Bradford, an excellent leader and popular man who earned the friendship and respect of everyone. He had been in post since 1890 so would have got to know Abberline at the Commissioner's Office quite well. Why did Bradford contact a private investigator rather than use his own officers? Perhaps because, after the Cleveland Street case, someone of Abberline's tact was needed; and the approach had come, not directly from a worried husband, but from a European embassy (which one, Abberline does not say).

Inventing bland names where he had to, Abberline was told that a Mrs Brown, living in South London, had gone missing. She had married 'a foreign gentleman' six months earlier and his business often took him abroad. Mrs Brown, who was almost fifty and apparently pregnant, received a telegram from the husband telling her of an accident that had befallen him on his arrival at an English port (we are not told which one, but the likelihood is that it was Dover). Mrs Brown's landlady helped her pack and saw her off to the station. That was the last that anybody in South London saw of Mrs Brown.

Her husband turned up ten days later, completely unharmed and unaware of the telegram that he was supposed to have sent. He contacted his country's embassy and the whole case was put in motion. Abberline began by talking to the landlady and discovered that Mrs Brown had received a large amount of cash two weeks before she had vanished. He was sure that this was not a 'domestic' – in other words the husband was innocent of any wrongdoing and genuinely shocked at his wife's disappearance. Tracing the source of the money, Abberline got a list of bank note numbers from the Bank of England, no doubt pulling ex-Scotland Yard strings to do so. Digging beneath the surface, Abberline met a raft of rumours from Mrs Brown's family, who were unsure about the foreign husband and the whirlwind romance. His own searches, however, were leading him in a different direction altogether, because six of the ten pound notes in Mrs Brown's possession turned up at the bank bearing the stamp of a South London post office.

Once again, Abberline used his connections with the Confidential Inquiry Department of the Post Office. He had worked with them on the Cleveland Street case and they were only too willing to help this time. They had to draw the line, however, at producing a copy of the original telegram that had arrived with news of 'Mr Brown's' fictitious accident; that could only be obtained with the permission of the sender. Even though he had not actually sent it, 'Mr Brown' was persuaded by Abberline to give his written permission, which he duly did.

In the meantime, the ex-chief inspector, armed with a photograph of Mrs Brown, went to the port to try to trace anyone who remembered her. He got the help of the local constabulary and combed the hotels and lodging houses in the town as well as talking to various employees of the railway. After two days, his enquiries paid off in a little cottage on the edge of town. The landlady there, whom Abberline calls Mrs Williamson, recognized the photograph as 'Mrs Green' and a quick reckoning of the dates made Abberline realize that she had turned up there on the day Mrs Brown had left London. He pursued the quite plausible line that the woman had mental issues which might explain her disappearance. The landlady 'pooh-poohed the idea' and over a glass of grog [Scotch] to which both she and Mrs Green were partial, she explained to the detective why Mrs Brown had come. She was due to meet someone 'for the purpose of adopting a baby from birth'. Abberline of course had come across baby-farming before, but he did point out to Mrs Williamson how odd this was as Mrs Brown was already pregnant. The landlady laughed and said, 'No such thing!'[8]

Something had clearly gone wrong with this adoption plan because Mrs Brown had left after a week giving no forwarding address. Mrs Williamson believed she had returned to London and before Abberline left in hot pursuit, he said how much he would like to return one day as he liked the place. The landlady came out with a genuine Victorian joke. 'Oh, you know I suppose that this is the place where they say an old man of ninety-eight was locked up by the police for throwing stones at his grandfather.'[9]

Back in London Mrs Brown's brother-in-law, who had offered to help in any way he could, was astonished by Abberline's findings. The detective, armed with 'Mr Brown's' permission to see a copy of the original telegram, made a careful tracing of it and realized it had been sent not from a port but from the East End of London.

Abberline had done well to get this far, but 'Mr Brown' was not impressed – 'I may have to say,' wrote Abberline, 'I got no credit from him' – and quite possibly no cash either, although Abberline does not comment on that. As for the information he had dug up, in the husband's view this was 'too idiotic to believe.'[10] It must have been quite painful for 'Mr Brown' to concede, when he saw Abberline's traced copy of the telegram, that it was in his wife's handwriting. She had sent the telegram to herself. 'Mr Brown' fainted.

This bizarre scene happened in the smoking room of a hotel, as Mr Brown could not bear to stay in the south London address with his wife gone – and Abberline seems relieved that no one saw the incident, which may be a fascinating insight into his psyche; grown men do not behave like that! Now there was movement in the recently-established bank account – withdrawals had been made over the last two days in the north London area. Abberline could now find that address and another genial landlady told him that 'Mrs Green' had taken two rooms in the house but had left three days before Abberline arrived. The detective showed her half a dozen photographs of women, one of which was Mrs Brown and she identified her immediately as Mrs Green. While staying there, she was very fond of her grog and had received several letters from people in connection with an adoption. There was no sign of pregnancy now and Abberline, with the brother-in-law in tow, tracked down the cabman who had taken her to the station, with a view to her travelling to Worthing. In fact there had been a last-minute change of plan and he had taken her instead to a house in the Richmond Road.

As a private investigator, Abberline's options were limited. He may have had useful police contacts but he had no powers of arrest nor right of entry to a house. Accordingly, he posed as a punter at the address in Richmond Road wanting to hire rooms on behalf of friends. He was shown into a 'very nice sitting room where I saw a lady and nurse apparently too busy attending to a baby to notice me.'[11] There were, no doubt, times when it was useful for a policeman or private detective to look like a bank manager.

Abberline had found the elusive Mrs Brown/Green, 'a buxom dame apparently in the best of health'. When Abberline told the brother-in-law about his discovery, the man said, 'Oh, if she has got a baby boy and can prove that it is her own, my children will be at least many thousands of pounds poorer.' Without going into details, it is obvious that Mrs Brown's family were less than straight with Abberline. In whatever trust her father had set up, the eldest *male* would inherit, so the brother-in-law's girls would be out of the financial picture.

The following Monday Mrs Brown returned to her south London home and told a delighted landlady that she had been kidnapped by 'some foreigners' and while in their clutches had given birth to the child she held in her arms. 'She had that day made her escape from them.'[12] Oddly, she had no idea of where she had been kept and there was no mention of a ransom note. Abberline was able to discover – from the landlady at Richmond Road – that the baby's nurse was actually his biological mother and that 'the poor girl had given birth to this illegitimate child.'[13] She was not only retained as a wet nurse but able to 'keep' the child for several weeks before being paid off with a lump sum.

The tale ended unhappily ever after. Mrs Brown lost the potential fortune, the respect of her friends and her husband, who left her and went to live abroad.

The single case highlights a number of points, especially the way Abberline operated. He would have had to adapt since leaving the police because he no longer had the warrant status that went with the job. That said, what we see him doing in the case of the vanishing lady must be what he did routinely throughout his career. He is clever and shrewd. His years on the force meant that he could sum up honesty or the lack of it quickly in anyone he met. He calls in favours from other officers and uses his contacts to circumvent red tape. He smarms his way round middle-aged, middle-class land-ladies and gets at least one of them tipsy on 'grog'. Above all, he gets results. We just wish we had more examples of his career in this period of his life.

If twenty-eight pages deal with the disappearance of Mrs Brown, only eleven cover his work at Monte Carlo. In a rare moment of poetry he wrote:

Monte Carlo is a paradise in some respects as the scenery combines sea and mountains with plenty of sunshine and [a] cloudless sky. Still you can catch a cold there before you know you have caught anything ...

Abberline spent three successive seasons, a total of twelve months, in Monte Carlo, which is likely to have been before 1898 (although he gives no dates). Monte Carlo (literally, Charles's Mountain) had its beginnings as a resort in the 1850s when the Grand Duke of Monaco, Charles III, granted a concession to two Frenchmen, Napoleon Langlois and Albert Aubert, to set up a curative sea-bathing business on the waterfront. Part of this establishment was a small casino on the lines of successful ones that had recently sprung up in Baden-Baden and Homburg. Gambling was illegal in various parts of Europe – Abberline himself records three cases of closing down illegal betting houses in his cuttings book – so Monaco represented a lawless 'naughtiness' which would be mirrored by Las Vegas in the years ahead.

The opening of the railway in 1868 brought the great and not very good of fashionable society and to make this rich elite feel at home, every comfort was laid on in terms of accommodation, food and champagne. The Hotel de Paris was built in 1864 and the Salle Garnier Theatre hosted the best in worldwide entertainment; the great actress Sarah Bernhardt appeared there as a nymph in an early production. The incredible casino building which Abberline would have known was opened in 1878, its fountained courtyards paved with marble and surrounded by twenty-eight onyx columns.

Fashionable society was ruled by 'the season'. In Abberline's London, this was a sophisticated cattle market between May and September when countless Victorian mamas would pay a fortune for balls and parties to introduce their marriageable daughters to eligible bachelors. Other than his tangential brush with this social class in the Cleveland Street scandal and a case in which he recovered jewels belonging to the Duke of Edinburgh (Queen Victoria's second son), Abberline can have had no experience of this stratified lifestyle which was way beyond his pocket. In Monte Carlo the 'season' was four or five months in the winter when rich and often titled punters got away from the chill of their homelands for the sunshine, luxury and money-making opportunities of the South of France.

Why was Abberline there at all? As he explains, 'The best and richest in Society can be seen there; also the lowest that can find money to get there.'[14] It was merely an extension of an observation made by Abberline's old boss, Thomas Arnold, when he retired from the Met the year after Abberline. Talking of the East End criminal, he said:

> You can still see your Fagins and your Nancies but Bill Sykes,[15] instead of resorting to a common lodging-house in Whitechapel or a thieves' kitchen, now lives in a luxurious country house, speaks two languages and plays tennis.[16]

English thieves had simply upped their game and their reputation in Monte Carlo was appalling. Abberline calls them 'the light-fingered gentry' and the British Vice-Consul there had been so inundated by complaints of theft that he had pressured the casino authorities into sending for Abberline. Again we have no clear idea as to how this happened, but again, it is likely to have been from Whitehall to Edward Bradford to the 'softly softly' approach of Abberline. On the occasions when serving Met detectives had been sent abroad – Littlechild, Andrews, Abberline himself – it was always for short periods because of the cost involved. Abberline would have been working on some kind of retainer, possibly funded by the casino itself.

We have no idea where Abberline – who spoke little or no French – stayed, but he was staggered by the extent of the robbery problem. 'I found I had got into a very hot shop'[17], surrounded by black-guards and thieves and he expected a team of five or six men to help. In fact he was on his own and put the word out that he was around. As a lifelong observer of human nature, and especially of the criminal classes, he could recognize a 'wrong 'un' sometimes on sight and no doubt did all he could to bolster this impression. Part of his problem was the reckless behaviour of the thieves' targets:

> The prude who, when at home, interferes with everybody else's business is a very different person there [Monte Carlo]. She is giddy and gay[18] and do not be surprised if you see her at the Café Riche dancing till the early hours in the morning with men and women just as naughty.

Abberline watched the clientele in the gaming rooms, the louche professional gamblers and the nervous ingénues. Two young ladies in particular caught his attention because wherever they went they had a huge male entourage which spent money on them like water. Abberline estimated that the jewels they were wearing were worth between £80,000 and £100,000 – an unbelievable sum in those days. These jewels appeared only at night and disappeared into hotel safes during the day, but the temptation to thieves must have been enormous. 'The countesses rubbed shoulders with cocottes [high class prostitutes] and noblemen and the elite of society elbow every rogue from all the sinks of Europe.'[19]

While expressing his exasperation – 'The world would no doubt be better off if such places as the gambling establishments were to disappear altogether' – Abberline is at pains to point out that the bank [i.e. the house] is straight as a die. Not so all the croupiers, and he recounts one incident in which he caught a croupier cheating and reported him to the casino authorities.

The only name which Abberline gives in his notes on Monte Carlo is that of Sam Lewis, who died in 1901. Lewis was a millionaire money-lender and philanthropist, originally from Birmingham, who spent about a month each year at the casino. He always made a maximum bid – 12,000 francs on the Trente Quarte table, where he ostentatiously threw bundles of notes over the heads of the crowd who flocked around him. Each time he won (he only ever bet on red at the roulette wheel) he would toss his cash on the ground knowing full well it would not be touched until the chef de partie had it all collected at the end of the evening. On one occasion, Lewis won £15,000 in an hour and the story appeared in the British Press next day. He asked Abberline how this had happened and Abberline told him the most likely source was the casino itself as a free advertisement. Lewis told him the downside; he estimated that overall, adding up his losses over the seasons, he was short to the tune of £80,000.

The sensational Press all over Europe carried stories of murders – as many as 200 a year – in Monte Carlo and a depressing string of suicides among those financially ruined by their huge debts. Abberline makes no comment on murder, but he does put the suicide angle into perspective. They were actually very rare indeed as the casino had a system called the Viaticum, actually used in the last rites in the Catholic church, which literally means 'provisions for the journey'. Cash was given to those financially embarrassed to get home. Obviously the monies had to be repaid eventually and Abberline concedes that suicides may have happened later as a result.

All this changed in 1898 when the man who caught the crooks at Monte Carlo took a job with the Pinkerton Agency. Allan Pinkerton had set up the world's most famous private detective organisation in 1850. A Scottish immigrant, he had served as a detective – its first – in the Chicago Police Department. The American Civil War saw the Agency change direction. In 1861 they foiled a plot to assassinate the new president, Abraham Lincoln, and so, almost by default, the Pinkertons became associated with national security. Throughout the war, Pinkerton men served behind the lines in a variety of capacities.

After 1865 the Agency became even more political, hiring itself out as strike-breakers and monitors of trade union activity, especially in the steel and iron and coal fields of Pennsylvania in the late 1870s. Their high-profile cases included the hunt for the outlaws Butch Cassidy and Harry Longbaugh (the Sundance Kid) in the

1890s and the catching of America's 'Jack the Ripper', H.H. Holmes (Herman Mudgett) in 1896.[20] Pinkerton himself died in 1884 but the Agency continued under his two sons.

Abberline's work with the agency, whose all-seeing eye logo formed their letterheads with the legend 'We never sleep', is currently a closed book, pending further investigation. All the Pinkerton records are lodged in the United States Library of Congress but unfortunately they are not sorted completely at present and so I have not been able to access them. They are partially available on microfiche but are not available online and no doubt a great deal of work has yet to be done on them. In a sense, the European and British branches of the Pinkertons were the forerunners of Interpol and mark the birth of international crime-solving cooperation.

It is clear that, in the beginning, the Pinkertons came to Abberline. Superintendent John Shore, four years older than Abberline, ran the Pinkerton's European branch until his death in 1898. He had only been in post for two years and William Pinkerton was not impressed with him. Since Shore had spent some time in the States and Canada in the 1880s infiltrating various Irish nationalist groups, it may be that he had come to the Pinkertons' attention then, since they were involved in similar work. Exactly why Abberline should have been chosen to fill the void left by Shore is not certain. Perhaps Shore had mentioned Abberline as a possible successor or perhaps they knew of the man's reputation from other sources.

One vague account has Abberline running the European end of the Pinkertons' operations for twelve years, which is unlikely. He travelled over Europe as a result, but had to resign in the end through ill-health – he does not give details. 'They however,' he wrote in his *Reminiscences*, 'sent me a very nice letter regretting it and congratulating me on the successful work I had done for them.'[21]

Chapter 12

A Policeman's Lot

We do not know exactly when Frederick Abberline hung up his handcuffs. He gives us no date for leaving the Pinkerton Agency, but it was probably before 1904 when he and Emma moved to Bournemouth on the south coast. The census of 1901 has them living at 313 Clapham Road in an imposing late-Victorian house that still stands. He was fifty-eight and Emma is listed as fifty-four, although this is at odds with the inscription on their grave. There is no profession or job listed for her and the likelihood is that she never worked. He is described as 'ex-Chief Inspector of Police'. On the day the census was taken, nine-year-old Harold Gibbons from Kensington was a visitor at No. 313, but who he was and what he was doing at the Abberlines' is unknown.

Two lodgers who would certainly have augmented Frederick's pension were a consulting engineer, Laurence Jones, and John Collis, a journalist who worked on the *Daily Telegraph* and the *Pall Mall Gazette*. Bearing in mind the interviews that Abberline gave two years later to the *Gazette* on the Klosowski/Chapman Ripper connection, it seems likely that his interviewer was either Collis himself or he had arranged it with a colleague. The last member of the household in Clapham was eighteen-year-old Mary Yates, who had come to the Abberlines from the Hanover Square workhouse.

Why did the Abberlines move to Bournemouth? At the time – and to an extent, still – it oozed gentility. Dotted among its pine trees are rows of respectable Victorian and Edwardian villas. The air was salubrious and it was a perfect retirement area for men who had spent their years in London's smog-laden atmosphere. Perhaps Frederick considered returning to Blandford, but his mother was long dead and his siblings lived in London's suburbs; it had been forty-one years since he had lived in the town and there was probably nothing left for him there.

Edmund Reid, the mercurial balloonist-cum-actor who had worked with Abberline on the Ripper case and challenged him over his views on Klosowski in 1903, had retired in 1896 to Herne Bay in Kent. Larger than life as ever, he got involved in local politics, clashed with vicars over the misuse of the Sabbath inevitable in a seaside resort, argued about the use of cesspools, and so on. He died of nephritis and cerebral haemorrhage on 5 December 1917 and the *Herne Bay Press*, to which he had often written in disgust, carried a fine obituary. He was 'a man of much geniality; he was a good companion and he could keep one interested for hours by reminiscences drawn from his long and varied experience.'[1]

By contrast, Abberline's retirement is marked by its total absence of information. The couple moved to 4 Methuen Road in 1904 (recently demolished to ease traffic) and to 'Estcourt', 195 Holdenhurst Road, just around the corner, in 1911. And for the next eighteen years, all is silence.

The ex-Ripper hunter probably bought his bread from the King's Bakery, directly opposite Estcourt; he may have drunk in the South Western Hotel. He almost certainly frequented the premises of local wine merchant Nelson Lees, who lived at No. 99, because Lees became the executor of his will. It may be that the Abberlines took in paying guests – Holdenhurst Road was at the heart of the town's guesthouse area, made lucrative by the railway and the relative nearness of London.

And that may explain the total anonymity of Abberline's last years. Bournemouth was much larger than Edmund Reid's Herne Bay and the notion of the illicit 'dirty weekend' for Londoners not wishing to be compromised left its mark, as at Brighton further along the coast. People kept to themselves. When I visited the museum in Blandford Forum, the curator there could immediately point out the shop run by the Abberlines. In Bournemouth, the only mention of the man is his three-line death notice, and the *Bournemouth Echo* even managed to get his rank wrong, calling him superintendent.

Ex-Chief Inspector Frederick Abberline died on 10 December 1929, his death registered by a Bella Huslling. The cause was bronchitis and heart disease. Yet even as he died, mystery and sudden death were not far away. The south coast had been lashed by terrible storms for days and on 9 December the body of a man from Bermondsey was found washed up on the beach. He was eventually identified by a missing finger. And a girl clerk had vanished into thin air. She was not answering her phone and her shoes had been found on a bridge in the town. Most mysteriously of all, as I read the *Echo*, was the banner headline – 'Ripper still at large'. It referred, of course, not to the Whitechapel murderer but the 'monster of Dusseldorf', Peter Kurten, then still unknown. Between February and November of that year he had sexually assaulted, raped or killed a total of twenty-nine people; alongside him, Jack was a beginner.

Eighty-six years on, the world that Frederick Abberline knew had changed beyond all recognition. A generation had been wiped out in the Great War and he and Emma had probably been lucky to escape the flu plague of the Spanish Lady that followed it. There were motor cars and telephones and radios, all the technology which might have stopped the Ripper in his tracks. Wall Street crashed two months before Abberline died, ushering in a worse recession in Britain than the one during which Abberline had been born. Pan-American airways were flying from the States to South America and the Graf Zeppelin airship had circled the world in twenty-one days. In the pictures, the twice weekly entertainment for the working classes, Alfred Hitchcock's *Blackmail* was the first all-talkie to be released in British cinemas. Werner Oland was the mysterious *Dr Fu Manchu* and Gary Cooper played *The Virginian*.

In the context of the Met, the Flying Squad had been going for ten years. Women Police Constables now had full powers of arrest. Field Marshal Julian Byng, a First World War hero, strode the corridors at the Yard as Commissioner and under him senior detectives had come to be known as the 'big five', greater celebrities than anyone in or out of uniform in Abberline's day.

The Ripper 'industry' which has made Frederick Abberline the most famous of all Victorian policemen today had not yet taken off. After a spate of pamphlets at the time of the killings, it all went very quiet until the Dutch writer Carl Muusmann wrote *Hvem Dar Jack the Ripper?* in 1908. The first book in English was Leonard Matters's

The Mystery of Jack the Ripper, published by Hutchinson in the year Abberline died; did he, I wonder, ever read it?

The Ripper hunter was buried in grave plot number Z250N in Wimborne Road Cemetery. It remained unmarked for years because Emma died three months later and there was no immediate family to set up a stone. Fast forward to 2001. For several years in the late 1990s, Australian John Grodl had been pestering Bournemouth Council for some kind of memorial to Abberline. By that time the Ripper industry was in full swing, with books, articles, television documentaries, movies, board games, even an opera – and yet the man most closely charged with catching him lay forgotten under a Bournemouth pine tree. Only the family could authorize such a memorial and no Abberline could be found, so the Cloak and Dagger Club stepped in. Today this fascinating and august group is called The Whitechapel Society and it does more than anyone else to explore every avenue (literally!) of the life and crimes of Jack the Ripper. The club held its biannual conference in Bournemouth in 2001 to help launch the placing of a plaque on Abberline's house at Holdenhurst Road and to place a headstone on his grave.

The plan was to have Johnny Depp to officiate, hot off the set of *From Hell*, but the actor was unavailable and Deputy Acting Commissioner John Grieve of the Met stepped in instead. On 29 September, with camera crews, Ripperologists, historians and even old Joseph Sickert in attendance, the blue plaque was unveiled. It reads:

> Estcourt – 195 Holdenhurst Road, the final home of Inspector [sic] Frederick George Abberline 1813 [sic!] – 1929. During his 29 years with the Metropolitan Police Abberline gained commendations and awards and became well-known for his work on the case of Jack the Ripper.

Two mistakes in five lines is not very impressive, but it is typical of the misrepresentations of the elusive Frederick Abberline, both in his lifetime and after it.

So what did Abberline leave behind? Today his name usually appears first, alphabetically, in any of the dozens of books on Jack the Ripper that appear each year. Despite his fame as the man in charge of detectives on the ground, no one has written a full book on the man until now. In the National Police Library at Bramshill in Hampshire is a curious reminder of the officer who hunted the world's greatest bogeyman. It is an ebony stick or cane, three feet long with a grotesque monk's head on its top. Around the neck is a silver collar inscribed 'Presented to Insp. Abberline as a mark of esteem by 7 officers engaged with him in the Whitechapel murders of 1888'. Exactly who these officers were is unknown and equally enigmatic is the head. It is a man's face in a monk's cowl and Ripper historian Donald Rumbelow has suggested that it might be a representation of 'Brother Martin', a monk who is said to have murdered a nun on the Mitre Square site in 1530 according to a booklet published by John Brewer in the year of the Ripper murders.

On the other hand, the case in which the cane is exhibited puts forward the theory that the hideous head may be a likeness of 'a Dr Alexander Pedachenko or Ostrog, a Russian anarchist living in the London area at the time'. Even with an object like this, the half-truths and the legends will not leave Abberline alone. The cane was presented to the Police College by Commander Ian Pirie, RN, whose father, Hugh, was acting superintendent in the Bournemouth Borough Police in the 1950s. How the cane got to Pirie Snr remains a mystery.

Abberline spent a mere eight months on the Ripper case in a police career that spanned thirty years and a life that spanned eighty-six. He was modest, conscientious, painstaking and methodical; all who knew him agreed with that. But he did not catch Jack – and like Jonathan Whicher, who failed to catch another cold-blooded killer, Constance Kent, his name and reputation will always be measured against that.

There are no mementoes on the Abberline grave today, but from time to time bouquets of flowers appear from well-wishers. One of these, left in 2011, bore a label which read:

Well, Fred, you know all the answers now and perhaps you always did. Sleep well, fellow copper.'[2]

Notes

Chapter 1

1. Extract from M.J. Trow, *Lestrade and the Dead Man's Hand*, London, Constable, 1992, pp. 15–16.
2. Denis Meikle, *Jack the Ripper – the Murders and the Movies*, Richmond, Reynolds and Hearn, 2002, pp. 163–4.
3. J Division, centring on Bethnal Green, was new in 1888. Of the Ripper victims, only Mary Anne (Polly) Nichols fell within their patch.
4. Having resigned from the Met in November 1888, Warren returned to the army and signally failed to distinguish himself in the Anglo-Boer war eleven years later.
5. Denis Meikle, *Jack the Ripper – the Murders and the Movies*, Richmond, Reynolds and Hearn, 2002, p. 187.
6. Notably: Paul Begg, Keith Skinner, Martin Fido, Donald Rumbelow and Philip Sugden.
7. Alan Moore, *From Hell*, Appendix, p. 23.
8. Denis Meikle, *Jack the Ripper – the Murders and the Movies*, Richmond, Reynolds and Hearn, 2002, p. 190.

Chapter 2

1. *The Domesday Book* (translation), Penguin, 2003.
2. Cottagers who were free men.
3. We know from first-hand testimony and photographs that little boys were often dressed as girls for the first three or four years of their lives, especially if there was no elder brother. Abberline may have got off lightly!

Chapter 3

1. Quoted in Martin Fido and Keith Skinner, *The Official Encyclopedia of Scotland Yard*, Appendix 4.
2. The colour was originally chosen by Peel so that the public did not associate the new force with the infantry's scarlet. He obviously overlooked the fact that the Light Cavalry wore dark blue and since Peel's own grandson served with the 11th Hussars, whose jackets were blue, this seems a little odd.
3. *Punch or the London Charivari*, 1847.

4. Arthur Munby was a barrister who spent most of his career in the Ecclesiastical Commissioner's Office. He had something of a fetish for working-class women, although he always denied any impropriety and made copious notes in his diary about female industrial workers. He secretly married Hannah Cullwick in 1873 although they had lived as man and wife for almost twenty years by that time. To his friends and family, she was merely his housekeeper; in private he often sat on her lap or she carried him from room to room.
5. Arthur Munby – Diary 20 February 1867.
6. Quoted in Martin Fido and Keith Skinner, *The Official Encyclopaedia of Scotland Yard*, p. 198.

Chapter 4

1. Title of an Irish patriotic song written *c.*1916 by Peardar Kearney, extolling the virtues of the Fenian Brotherhood – 'We may have great men, but we'll never have better; Glory O! Glory O! to the bold Fenian men.'
2. John Lindley, *Gardeners' Chronicle and Horticultural Gazette*; quoted in Cecil Woodham Smith, *The Great Hunger*, p. 35.
3. Quoted in Cecil Woodham Smith, *The Great Hunger*, p. 19.
4. Quoted in Cecil Woodham Smith, *The Great Hunger*, p. 19.
5. More men died in this conflict than in all America's other wars put together.
6. It was not new at all of course but a variant of what the ancient world knew as Greek Fire.
7. John Littlechild, *The Reminiscences of Chief Inspector Littlechild*, London, Leadenhall Press, 1894, p. 45.
8. The system of refusal to pay rent or do business with, the non-violent protest made by tenants of the land agent Capt C.C. Boycott in Ireland in 1880.
9. Nelson's Pillar, O'Connell St, Dublin, blown up by Irish republicans in 1966.
10. It is possible that this is PC Thomas Gallagher, 221H, who arrested the dangerous madman Charles Ludwig on 18 September 1888. He was dismissed in October 1890 for gossiping and drinking with a publican.
11. At that time the Tower of London had the largest collection of arms and armour in the world.

Chapter 5

1. London, Jack, *The People of the Abyss*, 1903, p. 24.
2. London, Jack, *The People of the Abyss*, 1903, p. 83.
3. Edwin Pugh, 'Slum-land' in *Living London*, 1913.
4. London, Jack, *The People of the Abyss*, 1903, p. 113.
5. The law (temporarily suspended sometimes in times of crisis) which states that a suspect must be charged with a specific crime within thirty-six hours or be released.
6. Toby, 1880s.
7. Several of Abberline's cuttings have no provenance in terms of newspaper article or date. I am assuming the year from various inferences.

8. A heavy cosh often made of bamboo and weighted with lead.
9. I.e. of material, rather than people!
10. Abberline's cuttings, *c*.1894.

Chapter 6

1. There would be a slight delay to this programme because of the discovery in September 1888 of a torso and separate legs found half buried in the site's basement. This was one in a series known as the Thames Torso Murders and the killer was never found.
2. All quotations in this section from the *East London Observer*, 17 December 1887.
3. Evidence given at inquest, quoted in Eddleston, p. 28.
4. Dew, *I Caught Crippen*, quoted in *A–Z*, p. 31.
5. Andrews seems to have stayed on in Canada for longer than was strictly necessary and it is possible that he was investigating the on-going problem of Irish Republicanism.
6. *Jack the Ripper Sourcebook*, p. 27.
7. This is the basis of the spurious case against James Maybrick, alleged in his fake diary (1992).
8. Quoted in Sugden, p. 162.
9. Pinhorn seems to have been something of a liability. Between 9 July and 8 November he was reprimanded three times, the first leading to a transfer from E to H Division.
10. Quoted in *Jack the Ripper A–Z*, p. 340.
11. Quoted in *Jack the Ripper: Scotland Yard Investigates*, p. 84.
12. Quoted in *Jack the Ripper: Scotland Yard Investigates*, p. 84.
13. He also kept a watching brief at various inquests into the Thames Torso cases in the 1880s.

Chapter 7

1. Most victims' clothing was black because that was the colour of mourning. The Victorians were obsessional about dressing correctly for funerals and such was the mortality rate among the poor that people like Liz Stride, with only one set of clothes, chose black as a matter of convenience.
2. Some people have found this odd, given the relatively short distances involved between Goulston Street and Mitre Square, but unless whistles were used (and they don't appear to have been since the City Force did not carry them) nothing would have alerted Long.
3. 'Open All Hours' applied to all sorts of establishments in the Abyss. There was a 24/7 culture which meant that the streets were constantly busy.
4. Some theorists have suggested that the non-appearance of Packer and another potential witness, Israel Schwartz, was a cunning ploy on the part of the police to withhold detailed information in order to catch the killer. This seems extraordinarily tortuous; Packer was a liar and Schwartz had very poor English, so the most obvious alternatives spring to mind.

5. These men were probably 'left overs' from Buffalo Bill Cody's Wild West Show that performed in London the previous year for Queen Victoria's Jubilee.
6. This was the main road to the Docks and the site, in 1811, of two linked murders, when the Marr and Williamson families were butchered. The crimes were never satisfactorily solved.
7. Mary Kelly Inquest, quoted in *Jack the Ripper; Scotland Yard Investigates*, p. 183.
8. *Morning Advertiser*, 7 December 1888.
9. Report by James Monro A49301G/1 quoted in *Jack the Ripper Sourcebook*, p. 427.

Chapter 8

1. As I write, the looting and riots across Britain (summer 2011) are said to be evidence of a 'moral collapse of society'.
2. Quoted in Fairclough, *The Ripper and the Royals*, London, Duckworth, 1992.
3. Fairclough explains this discrepancy by contending that Catherine Eddowes was not a Masonic victim and was killed by mistake because she had given the false name Mary Kelly at Bishopsgate Police Station on the night she died.
4. Quoted in Fairclough, p. 176.
5. Quoted in *Jack the Ripper A–Z*, p. 344.

Chapter 9

1. Today Hargrave Adam has an almost beatific reputation among some Ripper-ologists and the *Trial of George Chapman* (William Hodge, 1931) is a rare and expensive volume. He was an acquaintance of Robert Anderson, Charles Warren and Melville Macnaghten, and no doubt that gives him an edge most of us lack; but since the suspects of these men have now been discredited, this acquaintance is not much help.
2. *Cassell's Saturday Journal*, 28 May 1892.
3. *Forty Years of Man-Hunting*, London, Jarrolds, 1932, co-written by Edwin T. Woodhall.
4. *Pall Mall Gazette*, 24 March 1903.
5. *Pall Mall Gazette*, 24 March 1903.
6. *The Referee*, 29 March 1903.
7. *Pall Mall Gazette*, 31 March 1903.
8. All quotations from *The History of the Whitechapel Murders*, Anon, New York, 1888.
9. Of either the Middlesex Hospital or University College Hospital; it is unclear which.
10. *The Lancet*, 29 September 1888.
11. Tumblety was first put forward as a serious contender for the Whitechapel murders by Stewart Evans and Paul Gainey. He was a quack, conman and self-delusionist wanted in London on homosexual charges. The likelihood of him being the Ripper is extremely low.
12. *Pall Mall Gazette*, 24 March 1903.

13. The one exception is Liz Stride in Dutfield's Yard, who was lying twisted slightly to the right. The fact that the killer was disturbed pre-mutilation no doubt explains this.

Chapter 10

1. Quoted in Simpson, Chester and Leitch, *The Cleveland Street Affair*, p. 6.
2. PC Hankes' statement, quoted in *The Cleveland Street Affair*, p. 18.
3. Hansard, October 1889.
4. Quoted in *The Cleveland Street Affair*, p. 20.
5. Sladden is wrong on this. The cavalry regiments were divided into squadrons and troops, not battalions like the infantry.
6. Quoted in *The Cleveland Street Affair*, p. 49.
7. Quoted in *The Cleveland Street Affair*, p. 51.
8. *Pall Mall Gazette*, September 1889.
9. Quoted in *The Cleveland Street Affair*, p. 74.
10. Letter from Arthur Newton to DPP's office, 27 September, quoted in *The Cleveland Street Affair*, p. 81.
11. Quoted in *The Cleveland Street Affair*, p. 106.
12. Quoted in *The Cleveland Street Affair*, p. 107.
13. *The Cleveland Street Affair*, Little, Brown and Co., Boston-Toronto, 1976.
14. Nor could Superintendent Roy Ranson eighty-four years later when he tried to bring the 7th Earl of Lucan to court on a charge of murder. Some of Lucan's cronies frustrated the police at every turn.

Chapter 11

1. *Daily Telegraph*, 9 March 1891.
2. *Sunday World*, 10 May 1891.
3. *Pall Mall Gazette*, 4 January 1892.
4. *Daily Telegraph*, 9 June 1892.
5. *East London Observer*, 11 June 1892.
6. Cuttings Book.
7. I am enormously grateful to Paul Begg for allowing me access to this material.
8. Abberline's *Reminiscences*.
9. Abberline's *Reminiscences*, p. 12.
10. Abberline's *Reminiscences*, p. 16.
11. Abberline's *Reminiscences*, p. 25.
12. Abberline's *Reminiscences*, p. 27.
13. Abberline's *Reminiscences*, p. 27.
14. Abberline's *Reminiscences*, p. 1.
15. Charles Dickens' underworld had clearly been well established fifty years after *Oliver Twist* was written. Fagin was a Jewish 'fence' or receiver of stolen goods. Nancy (although Dickens never says so) was a prostitute; and Bill Sykes was a burglar.
16. *Eastern Post*, interview, February 1893.

17. Abberline's *Reminiscences*, p. 2.
18. In the sense of wild and irresponsible.
19. Abberline's *Reminiscences*, p. 4
20. Holmes was a contemporary of the Ripper, although he killed for financial gain and may have been responsible for twenty-seven murders in the Chicago area.
21. Abberline's Reminiscences, p. 41.

Chapter 12

1. *Herne Bay Press*, quoted in Nicholas Cornwell and Stewart P. Evans, *The Men Who Hunted Jack the Ripper*, p. 169.
2. Anon., 23 January 2011.

Bibliography

Anon., *The History of the Whitechapel Murders*, New York, Richard K. Fox, 1888.

Begg, P., *Jack the Ripper: the Definitive History*, Harlow, Pearson Education, 2005.

Begg, P. and Skinner, K., *The Scotland Yard Files*, London, Headline, 1992.

Begg, P., Fido, M. and Skinner, K., *The Complete Jack the Ripper A to Z*, London, John Blake, 2010.

Clack, R. and Hutchinson, P., *The London of Jack the Ripper: Then and Now*, Derby, Breedon Books, 2007.

Connell, N., *Walter Dew: The Man Who Caught Crippen*, Stroud, Sutton, 2005.

Connell, N. and Evans, S.P., *The Man Who Hunted Jack the Ripper*, London, Rupert Books, 2000.

Cornwell, P., *Portrait of a Killer: Jack the Ripper Case Closed*, London, Time Warner, 2003.

Evans, S. and Rumbelow, D., *Jack the Ripper: Scotland Yard Investigates*, Stroud, Sutton, 2006.

Evans, S. and Skinner, K., *Jack the Ripper: Letters from Hell*, Stroud, Sutton, 2001.

Evans, S. and Skinner, K., *The Ultimate Jack the Ripper Sourcebook*, London, Constable Robinson, 2001.

Fairclough, M., *The Ripper and the Royals*, London, Duckworth, 1992.

Fido, M. and Skinner, K., *The Official Encyclopaedia of Scotland Yard*, London, Virgin, 1999.

Gordon, R.M., *The American Murders of Jack the Ripper*, Westport, CT, First Lyons Press, 2005.

Hutchinson, P., *The Jack the Ripper Location Photographs*, Stroud, Amberley, 2009.

Leighton, D.J., *Ripper Suspect: the Secret Lives of Montague Druitt*, Stroud, Sutton, 2006.

Littlechild, J., *The Reminiscences of Chief Inspector Littlechild*, London, General Books, 2009 (originally published 1894).

McCormick, D., *The Identity of Jack the Ripper*, London, Arrow Books, 1959.

Meikle, D., *Jack the Ripper: The Murders and the Movies*, London, Reynolds and Hearn, 2002.

Moser, M., *Stories from Scotland Yard*, London, George Routledge, c.1893.

Moylan, J.F., *Scotland Yard and the Metropolitan Police*, London/New York, G.P. Putnam and Sons, 1929.

Simpson, C., Chester, L. and Leitch, D., *The Cleveland Street Affair*, Boston, Little, Brown & Co., 1976.

Sugden, P., *The Complete History of Jack the Ripper*, London, Robinson, 1995.

Trow, M.J., *Jack the Ripper: Quest for a Killer*, Barnsley, Wharncliffe, 2009.

Wilson, C. and Odell, R., *Jack the Ripper: Summing Up and Verdict*, London, Corgi, 1987.

Woodham Smith, C., *The Great Hunger*, London, NEL, 1970.

Unpublished sources

Abberline, F.G., *Reminiscences*, c.1904.

Abberline, F.G., *Cuttings*, c.1894.

Newspapers

Bournemouth Echo
Cassell's Saturday Journal
Daily News
Daily Telegraph
East London Observer
Eastern Post
Evening Standard
Lloyd's News
London Echo
Morning Advertiser
Pall Mall Gazette
Sunday World
The Times

Websites

www.casebook.org
www.jtrforums.com
www.whitechapelsociety.com

Index